Completely New

History of the World Cup

1930-2022

by

Paul Hawkins

Author

Paul Hawkins was an amateur footballer with Torquay United and Tooting and Mitcham before embarking on a banking career which took him to Brazil and the USA. He recently studied for a degree in History of Sport at Buckingham University, has been a keen student and supporter of football all his life, in particular the history of the FIFA World Cup from its commencement in 1930 and has attended some notable events, including the World Cup Final at Wembley in 1966 and the World Cup in Germany in 1974. He is the author of the books:

"The Key to Productivity and Performance"
"Career Management in the 21st Century."
"Football's First 100 Years, 1866 to 1966"
"Completely New History of the World Cup 1930- 2022"
"History of North and South American Football"
"Argentina Triumph in Qatar"

Contents

Foreword

Mission accomplished with following books so far:

"*Football's First 100 Years 1866-1966*, was published in the UK, in October, 2022 by Cambridge Scholars. It presents a history of football from an English perspective, starting with the consolidation and codification of early Football Association rules and the first recorded "modern" game of football in London in 1866, through to the English national team's victory in the 1966 World Cup.

This was followed by "*Argentina Triumph in Qatar,*" which contained match reports on all 64 matches in the sensational 2022 World Cup in Qatar.

Finally, the "*History of North and South American Football*" traces the ups and downs experienced by football administrators in some of the South and Central American countries together with the USA and Canada, which with the surge of interest generated by international competitions all over the world, have finally overcome initial financial issues and are now on a par with the rest of the world.

This book, "*Completely New History of the World Cup*" contains a review of each World Cup from the recent one in 2022 right back to the World Cup's origins in 1930, when four European football teams, representing their country, undertook a 20-day sea voyage by steamship to get to a destination, Uruguay, which would have been completely unknown to them. The players and officials who undertook the journey were courageous, maybe a bit crazy, but the experience would stay with them a lifetime.

Attending the 1966 and 1974 World Cups has caused me to look back in history to try to understand what makes a winner of this famous trophy. Was it the brilliance of the coach? Was it the presence of the most talented players, and how much luck is involved? Maybe a combination of all three. One well known journalist has written that the future winners of the World Cups are likely to be European coaches as they can best control the emotions of the players and also influence the players to respond to adversity. This could have been significant in the recent World Cup, when everyone's favourite team, Brazil, who had by far the most talented players, fell at the first hurdle when confronted with a penalty shootout. Was the pressure to score a goal to avoid penalties too much for them? Was the coach unable to manage the stress the players must have experienced?

A major influence for me has been the year I spent studying for a Master's Degree in History of Sport. The motivation came from two great sportsmen, Ed Smith, the Course Director, ex-England Test cricketer, writer and more recently England Cricket Selector and Simon Martin, Course Director, who has also authored sports books including "*Football and Fascism: The National*

Game under Mussolini", which was awarded a Lord Aberdare Literary Prize.

Other influences include the World Cups of 1950, 1954 and 1958 and the emergence of the greatest footballer the world had seen up to that time, Edson Arantes do Nascimento, better known as Pelé.

Not many football fans today have seen Pelé in his prime but just one statistic emphasizes his claim to fame. In the full year of 1958 when he appeared in the World Cup in Sweden at the age of 17, he played 46 games for Santos and scored 66 goals, most of the year still as a 17-year-old. Over the next four years Pelé played 151 games for Santos during which time he scored a total of 205 goals so, by the time he was twenty-one, he had scored over 200 league goals plus 26 for his country. I'm not sure any footballer can compete with that.

Single-handedly, he turned Santos, a little-known club until he arrived, into the best team in the world by virtue of two Inter-Continental Cup wins in successive years, defeating Inter Milan and Benfica.

Apart from reading every sports book I could get my hands on, the whole of my childhood and youth was spent playing football and cricket and I had ambitions to play professionally. Torquay United (before being condemned to non-league football) approached me as a 16-year-old and I trained with them in the evenings whilst still at school and played for their youth team and reserves until the age of 21. There followed two years with Tooting & Mitcham in the Isthmian League.

This is where I earned my first *"boot"* money as ironically you could earn as much in those days playing for the leading amateur clubs than for a professional football league team. But if you didn't play well, you didn't get paid of course.

The education I received at Torquay Grammar School and one year at Leeds University, taught me that there were other things in life besides football and cricket and at the age of twenty-three, I gave up my sporting ambitions. It was just a decision young people make and you just get on with it.

I decided to go to London to seek a career outside sport and I took up banking and within a year I was flying with the now defunct airline Varig on the way (ironically) to Santos, the coffee port in Brazil to join The Bank of London and South America where I used to watch the Santos football team play.

Wherever I went, New York, Portugal, Kuwait, Saudi Arabia, Dubai, I always found time to play football. In Kuwait, we engaged with a number of ex-football league players who were coaching local clubs. Our 5-a-side football team included George Armstrong, ex-Arsenal, Jimmy Melia of Liverpool and England, Malcolm Crosby, ex-York City, who later coached Sunderland to the FA Cup Final, and for those who participated, it was a regular lesson in how to play football. In summary, this is a book written by someone whose childhood love of sport has never left him.

The World Cup of today has taken on a new meaning all over the world. FIFA has suffered from frequent investigations into its bidding process but it has succeeded in transforming the World Cup from a small event limited to countries which have the required finances to the mammoth event today, which has not only reached out to footballing nations all over the world, but has also transformed it into an event which turns over massive sums of money in terms of sponsorship and marketing rights.

The 2022 World Cup has been a spectacular event. We have all witnessed a display of footballing skills at the highest level played at state-of-the-art stadiums by players who have had the benefit of luxurious accommodation and training facilities. We have followed teams from the group stages, playing for the necessary points to qualify them for the knock-out stages, thence to the very essence of the World Cup when two teams fight to the death, with the loser taking no further part in the tournament. Triumph and disaster in every match with the careers of team coaches hanging by a thread.

The final was a match which has been labelled one of the greatest matches in the history of football, with two of the most talented footballers of their generation displaying all their skills from the kick-off right through to the 120th minute, followed then by the dreaded penalty shoot-out, which culminated in triumph for the winners and absolute devastation for the losers.

Finally, many congratulations to the Qatari World Cup Organising Committee for creating an incredibly entertaining tournament. The Qatari players, fans and officials will remember this World Cup with great pride and their players will have earned their place in their nation's history books.

Introduction

*"Jules Rimet, pioneer of the World Cup, soon to become
the greatest sports event in history."*

World Cup origins

Jules Rimet was ambitious. He was responsible for
driving FIFA, which was formed in 1904, much to the
chagrin of the Football Association, from a sleepy
organisation, in its earlier years, to the dynamic force the
footballing world witnessed in the 1920s and 1930s. In
1914, FIFA agreed to recognise the Olympic football
tournament as a world championship, and following
WW1, the 1920, 1924 and 1928 Olympic Games staged
the first truly international football tournaments.
However, the Olympics was only for amateur
competitors and many footballing nations in Europe had
already formed professional leagues, so to recognise this
development, something had to change.

On May 26th, 1928, FIFA met in Amsterdam and
decided to organise its own international, professional
football tournament. FIFA moved quickly, without the
bureaucracy that exists today, and a year later met in
Barcelona to elect the host country for the first World
Cup in 1930. After much debate, FIFA gave way to
Uruguay, who tabled the most convincing bid and
seemed to have the finance and determination to host the
event. Uruguay at that time was a small insignificant

country with a population of scarcely 2 million and, for FIFA, it was a shot in the dark, the only risk they were to take in 60 years of selecting host countries, apart, perhaps, from the 1978 World Cup hosted by Argentina, which took place in the throes of a military revolution.

Little did they know what they had started

However, it worked, after initial reluctance by European countries to support the Uruguayans, four countries, Belgium, France, Rumania and Yugoslavia, agreed to participate and undertake the two-week sea voyage to South America. Argentina, Brazil, Paraguay, Peru, Chile, Bolivia, Mexico and the USA joined Uruguay in what has become a historic event. Little did these nations know what they had started and what lay in store for the World Cup over the next 90 years.

What if… …

If the 1930 World Cup had not taken place, this would definitely not have been the end of it. FIFA's next attempt would have been to stage the World Cup in Europe and it would have gone ahead with or without the South Americans. Eventually, with the advent of inter-continental air travel, they would have seen the benefit in taking part in what would still have been the first global professional football tournament. The South Americans all have passion, pride and an inbred desire to display their talents and they would all have wanted to do it not just in their own back yard but also on the global stage, not forgetting, of course, Argentina and Uruguay had both travelled to Europe for the 1924 and 1928 Olympic Games.

Disruptive events

It has not all been smooth running in the World Cup. There was a massive earthquake in Chile in 1960, two years before their World Cup. There was a violent military revolution in Argentina where thousands of Argentinians were massacred but the football went ahead and by winning the World Cup, it allowed the host country an opportunity to wash themselves clean of the darkest period in their history. The 1982 World Cup took place just a few weeks after the Falklands War had ended. England and some of their European allies were about to pull out of the World Cup, if it had not ended when it did. To play football in the host country with whom they were at war, was, of course, inconceivable.

Scandals

Later, there have been regrettable scandals concerning the bidding process for the World Cup. FIFA has been investigated and a number of arrests have been made of FIFA representatives in different parts of the world. The stain of these incidents will stay with FIFA forever. It became clear, in the investigations, that FIFA was an organisation with no governing body. Despite this dark period in their history, FIFA's greatest achievement is undisputable. They have initiated, developed and transformed the World Cup into the greatest event in the history of sport.

Qatar, the hosts for 2022

"Throughout the tournament the Qatari team will benefit from tumultuous support from excitable fans for whom this is an iconic event, the memory of which will be treasured for a lifetime."

Qatar declared its independence from its status as a British protectorate in September, 1971, preferring to remain separate from the trucial states that became the UAE. In the last twenty years, increasing oil and gas revenues have brought prosperity and social progress and there has been massive investment in the country's infrastructure. The city of Doha, for example, with its iconic high-rise buildings and skyscrapers is unrecognisable from the small town of fifty years ago.

Qatar was announced as the host of the 2022 World Cup at a FIFA Congress in Zurich in December, 2010. They successfully held off the USA in the final round of bidding and USA were later awarded the 2026 World Cup in a joint-bid with Canada and Mexico. This is the first time the World Cup is to be staged in the Middle East and only the second time in Asia, following the 2002 World Cup held in Japan and South Korea.

Football in Qatar was first introduced in the 1940s and continued to develop in parallel with the expansion of the national economy. The Qatar Football Association was established in 1960 and Qatar became members of

FIFA three years later. Algeria, Morocco, Saudi Arabia, Tunisia, Kuwait, Iraq, Iran, Egypt, Iraq and UAE have all qualified for the World Cup before, but this is the first time Qatar has appeared.

In the 1970s, Qatar built the Khalifa International Stadium, which would become the iconic venue for many leading football matches over the next thirty years. The stadium will be hosting several matches in the 2022 World Cup including Netherlands v Ecuador, England v Iran, Germany v Japan and the 3rd place play-off.

The World Cup Final, however, will be held at the Lusail Iconic Stadium in Lusail, 20 kilometres north of Doha, which was completed in 2021. During the 2022 World Cup, nations featuring at the stadium will include Brazil, Argentina, Portugal and Saudi Arabia as well as other teams who make it to the knock-out stage of the tournament.

Qatar has invested heavily in its youth teams and the highlight of their youth team performances was finishing runner-up to Germany in the 1981 tournament, held in Australia. The team reached the final after defeating Brazil and England. Qatar has hosted the Arabia Gulf Cup tournament three times and won the event in 1992 and 2004. Qatar also beat hosts Saudi Arabia in the 2014 Arabian Gulf Cup final.

Their most impressive performance of all was probably winning the football gold medal at the 2006 Asian Games with a 2-0 victory over Iraq in the final. A young

Qatari side impressed with great attacking football in front of packed stadiums right throughout the competition. Most of the players from the gold medal-winning team went on to serve the senior team for a number of years.

For the World Cup in 2022, Qatar have a good chance of progressing from their group consisting of Netherlands, Senegal and Ecuador. Throughout the tournament they will benefit from tumultuous support from excitable fans for whom this is an iconic event, the memory of which will be treasured for a lifetime. They will also benefit from considerable investment in their youth teams over the past fifteen years and a coach, Felix Sanchez, who has been working with teams of different age groups since 2013, which makes him the longest serving coach for any of the national teams.

It has been a long journey for Qatar and the time has now arrived for them to showcase what has become the world's most popular and heavily-marketed sports tournament.

Opening day fixtures

"In the 1930 World Cup, the first goal scorer was clearly going to make history. The honour fell to Lucien Laurent who scored for France in 19th minute of the first World Cup match against Mexico on 13th July, 1930, which France finally won 4-1."

After seemingly an age of preparation, the Qatar World Cup 2022 is about to get underway. The new stadiums have been completed, match tickets have all been sold and the sponsors will be hoping they achieve a good return on their investments. For the first time in 92 years, every match will take part in or nearby Qatar's capital city of Doha. This has only happened once before in World Cup history and that, of course, was in Uruguay's capital city of Montevideo in the very first World Cup in 1930.

Smallest cities

Qatar shares another unique feature with Montevideo. They are the smallest cities that have hosted the World Cup. In 1930, Montevideo was home to scarcely 250,000 inhabitants. In 2022 the official population of Doha was 900,000. Another interesting statistic is that when Brazil staged the first post-war World Cup in 1950, the population of Qatar was just 25,000. Since then, of course, oil and gas discoveries have turned Qatar into one of the wealthiest countries per capita in the world and now boast state-of-the-art high-rise office blocks and luxurious residential buildings which contribute to create an incredible skyline.

First up, Qatar v Ecuador

So, what awaits us in the first match, historically featuring the host country? Qatar and Ecuador have met on just one previous occasion, on 12th October, 2018 at the Jassim bin Hamad stadium in Doha, a game which Qatar won 4-3. Goals were scored by Akram Afif, Almoez Abdulla (2), and Hassan Al Haydos for Qatar and Enner Valencia (2) and Francisco Cevallos for Ecuador.

Akram Afif, Karim Boudiaf, Bassam Al Rawi, Pedro, Hassan Al Haydos and Boualem Khoukhi who start in today's match, all featured in the match in 2018 and Enner Valencia, Ayrton Preciado, Jhegson Mendez and Luis Cacedo, who start for Ecuador, all played in the previous match. Several players from each side will remember this game and will know that it will be a tough encounter today.

Lucien Laurent makes history

The initial fixtures in the World Cup have produced some interesting matches. In 1930, the first goal scorer was clearly going to make history. The honour fell to Lucien Laurent who scored for France in 19th minute of the first World Cup match against Mexico on 13th July, 1930, which France finally won 4-1. Interestingly, Monsieur

Laurent, who naturally had no idea at the time of the significance of the goal, lived to the age of 97 and was the last survivor of the 1930 World Cup.

Just Fontaine record

There then followed a period of high scoring in the opening fixtures. Italy defeated USA 7-1 in 1934 and they were the first team on their way home as there were no group games in 1934, the only time this has occurred. Brazil defeated Mexico 4-0 in 1950 and this was followed by a repeat of this fixture in 1954 when Brazil went one better and won 5-0. In 1958, France did even better defeating Paraguay 7-3, with the legendary Just Fontaine scoring a hat-trick towards his total of 13 in this World Cup which has never been equalled.

England v Uruguay, 1966

The England v Uruguay scoreless draw in 1966 was the start of a succession of scoreless draws, right up to the 1978 World Cup in Argentina. The remaining opening fixtures have consisted of a number of the weaker teams so there have been no surprising results and both teams tend to be a little cautious as to lose the first game can be the commencement of a painful journey ending in a quick exit. The last time two leading teams met in the opening fixture was, in fact, the England v Uruguay match. England, the eventual winners, were playing against a team that had already won the World Cup on two occasions

2022 World Cup

Qatar

"From humble beginnings in Montevideo to the majestic stadiums of Doha, a roller-coaster journey lasting 92 years."

Qatar was announced as the host of the 2022 World Cup at a FIFA Congress in Zurich in December, 2010. They successfully held off the USA in the final round of bidding and USA were later awarded the 2026 World Cup in a joint-bid with Canada and Mexico. This is the first time the World Cup is to be staged in the Middle East and only the second time in Asia, following the 2002 World Cup held in Japan and South Korea.

By the evening of 18th December, 2022, we had enjoyed one of the most exciting World Cups in history, full of surprises, an incredible display of talent throughout and a breathless run by Morocco, which has earned them a few million more fans and brought stardom to a number of players, virtually unknown to us before the World Cup. To think it all started in 1930 with thirteen teams, four of them from Europe making a two-week sea voyage by steamship to get to a destination most of the players would never have heard of, Montevideo, a city with a population of scarcely half a million people. They had no idea what they had started and what would develop very quickly into the world's greatest sporting event.

Full circle Montevideo to Doha

After an amazing roller-coaster journey of 22 World Cups held in every major city, Rome, Paris, Rio de Janeiro, Bern, Stockholm, Santiago, London, Mexico City, Munich, Buenos Aires, Madrid, Pasadena, Tokyo, Seoul, Johannesburg and Moscow, we have arrived, full circle, 92 years later, in the city of Doha, Qatar with a population of, once again, scarcely one million people.

Stadiums

The organisers have constructed the most amazing stadiums, created the most luxurious accommodation and training centres for the teams and 64 football matches went ahead with scarcely a blemish. There were no major incidents involving the players or coaches, and officials from every corner of the globe operated with remarkable efficiency. Of course, there were some disputes over some refereeing decisions and VAR. Some blatant fouls were overlooked and from time-to-time errors were made, but that is part of football.

First matches

The first match took place at Al Bayt Stadium on 20th December, and featured the host team, Qatar, against Ecuador, one of the surprise qualifiers from the tough South American group. To the disappointment of the Qatari fans, who had waited a long time for this match, it did not go according to plan and the Ecuadorians won with ease. Football is a game of different levels and it was a signal to the Qataris that the playing standard of some of these teams was on a slightly higher level than they were used to. The other matches they played had similar results but their squad of players and officials will have all benefitted from the experience of playing on the global stage and writing their names into the World Cup history books. Netherlands and Senegal eased their way through to the quarter-finals from that group.

"Volte face" for the Spanish

Spain set standards of their own with an early 7-0 victory over Costa Rica, but in amazing turnaround, they lost to South Korea in their group and barely qualified for the next stage but then disaster of all World Cup disasters, after 80% possession in the Round of 16 match with Morocco, they slipped into the dreaded penalty shoot-out and failed to score one penalty, each player trying to do something clever instead of shooting with power.

England survive

England also started well with a 6-2 victory over Iran, Gareth Southgate setting standards for himself by questioning why the team gave away two goals. They followed up this win with a 0-0 draw with USA, whose energy and determination qualified them for the quarter-finals along with England, but USA went out to

Netherlands in the Round of 16 with England defeating Senegal 3-0.

Plenty of shocks

The shock of the tournament so far has been the elimination of Germany and Belgium, two of the fancied teams, Germany due to a defeat by Japan and Belgium going down to Cameroon. One of the features of this tournament has been the suspense created in the final group games where qualification was literally decided in the last few moments of the matches.

France and Brazil looking good

France, another fancied team, strolled through their group and again in the Round of 16 game against Poland, who have unfortunately become a one-man team with their survival down to a good performance by Robert Lewandowski, who on this occasion, failed to deliver.

Brazil were the star team in the early stages and their football was a delight to behold, creating movements which left opponents rooted to the spot. It will take a very good performance to beat them and they are the odds-on favourites to win their sixth World Cup trophy.

Argentina are slowly improving after a shock defeat to Saudi Arabia, whose midfielder, Salem Al Dowsari, scored the goal of the tournament, so far.

Quarter-finals

So, the quarter-final draw looks like this:

Croatia v Brazil at Education City Stadium
Netherlands v Argentina at Lusail Iconic Stadium
Morocco v Portugal at Al Thumama Stadium
England v France at Al Bayt Stadium

Match officials

There have been some stand-out referees who will be in line to officiate at the World Cup Final. Contenders will probably be: Ismail Elfath of USA, Cesar Ramos of Mexico, Fernando Rallapini of Argentina, Anthony Taylor of England, Szymon Marciniak of Poland and Clement Turpin of France.

Contentious decisions

There have been some heart-breaking decisions. Did Kaoru Mitoma of Japan get to the ball before it crossed the line and then hooked the ball into the goalmouth for the goal against Spain that eliminated Germany from the World Cup? VAR said yes and that was it.

Uruguay were leading Ghana 2-0 but needed another goal to qualify for the quarter-finals. In the last minutes of the game, Edinson Cavani's legs became entangled with a Ghana defender's. He went over, the penalty claim looked legitimate but no penalty was given and Uruguay were out. This was just the group stage and we knew there were going to be more contentious decisions from the match officials including VAR, some affecting the result. This has happened since time immemorable.

Potential winners?

Argentina, Brazil, France, Portugal and England were the stand-out teams to make it through to the quarter-finals. Brazil played exhilarating football against the South Koreans who seemed in a state of shock after they conceded four goals in the first half. Mbappe scored two outstanding goals to overcome the stubborn defence of Poland and England produced three quality goals by the 60th minute to defeat Senegal. Portugal put on a fantastic show against Switzerland and Ronaldo's replacement, Gonçalo Ramos, helped himself to a hat trick in his first World Cup appearance in their 6-1 win.

Dark horses

Netherlands, as before are the dark horses. They are slowly improving but have yet to reach the standards we expect from the finalist in 2010 and the semi-finalist in 2014. The match against Messi and his Argentinian team, like all the other quarter-final matches should be great viewing whether you are at one of these magnificent stadiums in Doha, watching from one of the thousands of fan zones all over the world or sitting in comfort by the TV. A win for Argentina would be a triumph for one of the greatest players in the world who has literally dragged his team through each round.

Brazil's shock exit

The Samba kings were looking good in their quarter-final match against Croatia. A brilliant goal by Neymar looked to have sealed a win but Bruno Petkovic equalised in the dying moments. Croatia scored all four of their penalties and Rodrygo missed his, so Brazil, tournament favourites for a long time, are out. They will be regretting all those missed chances. The Brazilian motto has always been in the past no matter how many you score, we will score more and up to the Croatia match, it had worked out well but as we know in the World Cup, you cannot afford a lapse in concentration and that's what happened to Brazil. They were hoping this World Cup would have been an opportunity to erase memories of the match all Brazilians try to forget – the 7-1 drubbing by Germany in the 2014 World Cup, in their own back yard, but they will have to wait another four years, like a lot of other teams, 31 in fact.

Argentinians and the French both chasing their third World Cup

Argentina's first win in 1978 was amazingly staged during a military revolution where thousands of Argentinians were massacred. In 1986, their victory was stained by Maradona's "Hand of God" goal, but redeemed by the greatest goal in World Cup history. Well, they are now favourites to win their third World Cup as they have reached the semi-finals and face Brazil's conquerors, Croatia.

France are also chasing their third World Cup, having previously won in Paris, defeating the mighty Brazilians, and also in Moscow, dealing a deadly blow to the surging Croatians and now in Doha, having overcome the devastated England team in a feisty encounter at Al Bayt Stadium. The game was marred by an incompetent display of refereeing by the Brazilian Wilton Sampaio, who overlooked a number of obvious infringements, one leading to France's first goal and another a foul on Kane on the edge of the penalty area. England had their chance to even it up, but Harry Kane blasted his penalty high and wide, recalling Chris Waddle's similar penalty in the 1990 penalty shoot-out.

England coach faces a grilling

England will now face a barrage of criticism, questioning how a team with so many talented players can't make it past the last eight and given scores of opportunities against France why they could not manage to score more than just one goal (from a penalty kick.) Also, the star of England's team was Bucayo Saka who gave Theo Hernandez a torrid time on the right wing. Inexplicably, he was replaced in 79th minute when he could have done further damage in the closing 10 minutes (plus 8 minutes added time), and maybe in extra-time if it got that far. In his place Southgate brought on Raheem Sterling, who had just returned from a trip to the UK and who could scarcely get his foot round the ball. Question marks also hover over his team selection, in particular, of Jordan Henderson, when it is clear, despite his excellent service over the years and despite having a good season with Liverpool, that he can no longer play at this level. Maybe he was included to help Kyle Walker look after Mbappe but Walker did well to contain him on his own.

Everybody's favourite second team

There is usually one unheralded team that struggles its way to the semi-finals. This time it was Morocco, who are becoming everyone's favourite second team. After defeating Belgium in the group stage, they defeated Spain in the Round of 16 and then caused the biggest upset in the tournament so far, eliminating Portugal in the quarter-final. They scored a brilliant headed goal by En-Nesyri with goalkeeper, Diogo Costa left punching thin air. They then just packed their defence with one oversized defender after another coming on as subs. At times all 11 players were in the penalty area. Whether you can win the World Cup with this strategy remains to be seen.

So far, this has been an exceptionally friendly World Cup without any unsavoury incidents except for a rather unpleasant clip of the Argentinian players mocking the Dutch players as they sat, fatigued and devastated after losing out on penalties. Lionel Messi was also seen approaching the Netherlands coach, Louis Van Gaal in a threatening manner, for what reason we don't know.

Semi-finals

Argentina v Croatia at Lusail Iconic Stadium
France v Morocco at Al Bayt Stadium

Argentina well prepared

Having survived an early loss to Saudi Arabia, Argentina have improved with every performance, and fortunately for them, Messi seems to be getting more involved with every game he plays. Croatia were simply no match for Argentina. Having gone behind early on, they were always struggling and although they had more possession, they were unable to making any impact up front. Messi scored from a penalty and Manchester City's Julian Alvarez scored one of the best individual goals of the tournament, running from his own half until he found himself one on one with goalkeeper Dominik Livakovic, one of Croatia's heroes on their journey to the semi-finals and Alvarez made no mistake. Messi then turned on his own brand of magic and twisted and turned past Josko Gvardiol before crossing for Alvarez to score his second goal. 3-0. Game set and match and into the final for the sixth time.

France in the final

France had a tougher match and were never at ease against a very skilful Moroccan team that have been both the surprise and delight and of the tournament. Like Argentina, France scored early through Theo Hernandez but this did not stop Morocco and they went close on numerous occasions, before Kolo Muani scored a further late goal to finish it, just a few minutes after coming on as a sub. 2-0 and well deserved but congratulations to Morocco on a fantastic tournament, defeating Belgium, Spain and Portugal on the way to their first World Cup semi-final.

Argentina v France

So, an intriguing final Argentine v France. Head-to - head: Argentina 6 France 3. The most recent match was in the 2018 World Cup in Russia, the Round of 16 encounter in Kazan, which France won 4-3 by virtue of goals from a penalty by Griezmann, Pavard's goal of the tournament and two goals by Mbappe. Argentina replied with goals from Di Maria, Mercado and Aguero.

Argentina two up after 20 minutes

Right from the start Argentina demonstrated their superiority. In the first 15 minutes, their midfield took complete control of the match with Di Maria the ace card. Kounde was unable to cope with his skilful play and time and time again, he led movements towards the French goal. He clearly wasn't in Deschamps plans as Di Maria hadn't started in any of the other matches. Then came the killer blows. Firstly, he waltzed around Dembele, who reacted like any, young inexperienced player would, had a rush of blood and tripped Di Maria. Penalty. Messi scores 1-0.

Ten minutes later a move of sheer brilliance from
Argentina which will be talked about for many years.
From Montiel to MacAllister to Alvarez with the final
ball being swept out to Di Maria and he doesn't miss
these. 2-0 and it was looking bleak for France.

Shocks. Otamendi trips Muani. Penalty. Mbappi scores
1-2. Two minutes later. Thuram to Mbappe and he
scores with a great volley 2-2. Game on. End-to-end
stuff now. Chances at both ends with France with their
tails up. Mbappe shoots over the bar. Goalmouth
scramble. Martinez saves. 90 minutes up. 8 minutes
stoppage time. Another chance for France. Another
scramble. Messi knows he gave away the second goal
and he's probably thinking about it. Messi shoots. Lloris
saves. Extra time. Chances at both ends. Miraculous
escapes for both teams. Messi scores following another
great move 3-2. Handball by Montiel. Penalty scored by,
who else, Mbappe.

Match of the highest quality

Penalties. Mbappe scores, Messi scores, Coman misses,
Dybala scores, Tchouameni misses, Paredes scores, Kolo
Muani scores, Montiel scores the winner and the
pulsating match ends in victory for Argentina. In 21
World Cups the best team has won in 90% of the
tournaments and this was no exception. Argentina just
got better and better as the tournament progressed and
their first half performance was quite unbelievable. They
took their foot off the pedal in the second half and

France got back into the game with a virtuoso display by Mbappe, who was well marshalled in the first half. At 2-2, they could have scored again which may have changed things and even at 3-3 in the closing minutes of the match Thuram, who was a handful, had another opportunity saved by the goalkeeper of the tournament, Aston Villa's Emiliano Martinez, who is sure to receive a hero's welcome when he returns to Villa Park next week.

Players we have watched, players we have missed

Finally, over the past 22 World Cups we have been able to watch or read about some amazing footballers, Pelé, Garrincha, Maradona, Puskas, Messi, Cruyff, Ronaldo of Brazil, Ronaldo of Portugal, Figo, Ronaldinho, Rivaldo, Rooney, Lineker, Gascoigne, Muller, Charlton, Rivellino, Rossi, Vieira, Shevshenko, Zidane and most recently Kylian Mbappe and many more but spare a thought for George Best, Alfredo Di Stefano, Duncan Edwards, David Ginola, Sami Hyypia, Liam Brady, Ian Rush, Eric Cantona, George Weah, Tommy Taylor, Ryan Giggs, Jim Baxter, and finally members of the famous Torino team, who had just won four Serie A league titles, seven of whom were in the Italian squad for the 1950 World Cup, before losing their lives in an air crash in 1949. All of these players, some of them amongst the very best in the world, had one thing in common. They were not in the right place at the right time and were not lucky enough to be able to display their talents on the grandest stage of all, the FIFA World Cup.

Watershed moment

With England losing 2-1 but having more possession and constantly threatening the French goal, it looked like they finally had an opportunity to level the score when Theo Hernandez blatantly fouled Mason Mount in the 84th minute and a penalty was awarded to England. Memories of the penalty shoot-out against Germany in the semi-final of the 1990 World Cup immediately sprung to mind but surely not again. In 1990 Chris Waddle's penalty was said to have travelled "high into the sky, bounced onto the athletics track nearby and landed in the safe hands of a spectator." Well, Harry Kane wasn't born until 1993 so he couldn't have witnessed Waddle's spot-kick but he did his very best to emulate it as it went in exactly the same direction as Waddle's and ended up in the grateful hands of a French spectator sitting somewhere in the 10th row behind the goal. England's opportunity to appear in their first World Cup final for 56 years had once again been snatched from them. Ten minutes later the England players left the field in a familiar picture of doom and gloom.

Winning coach

Lionel Scaloni

Scaloni played most of his football career in Spain and won the Spanish League title with Deportiva La Coruña in 1999/2000, the only time the club has won the league title. He played for Deportiva for eight years including a loan period with West Ham United. He has been associated with the Argentinian national team since 2017 as assistant coach and coach for the U20 squad, taking over as their national team coach in 2018 following the World Cup in Russia. He had immediate success in the Copa America and the Argentinian team won the trophy in 2021 for the fist time in 28 years.

Scaloni has so far won 41 out of 61 Argentina matches played, which is a win-ratio of over 67%. Since taking over, Argentina have only lost five matches. In the World Cup in Qatar, he managed to overcome a dismal display against Saudi Arabia in the very first game and then win the next six matches en route to the unforgettable World Cup final. Probably his biggest achievement was in driving Lionel Messi and his colleagues to perform at the highest level when it was required in the tough semi-final against Croatia and the final itself against France. The football Argentina played in the final was some of the best ever witnessed in a World Cup final and Scaloni has taken much of the credit.

Lionel Scaloni has written his name into World Cup history as the 21st coach to win the World Cup since

Alberto Suppici's triumph with Uruguay in 1930 which was followed by Vittorio Pozzo's double in 1934 and 1938.

2022 World Cup Final

18th December 2022

Lusail Iconic Stadium, Doha

Argentina 3 France 3

(Argentina win 4-2 on penalties

2018 World Cup

Russia

"La France une fois de plus"

"Vladimir Putin officially declares the opening of the World Cup on 14th June, 2018. This was followed by hit songs from Robbie Williams, who then sang a duet with Russian soprano, Aida Garifullina and the 2018 World Cup was underway."

Russia hit the ground running

Russia started off their World Cup campaign with an encouraging 5-0 win over Saudi Arabia, in Moscow. They also defeated Egypt 2-1 in Volgograd but lost to Uruguay 3-0 in Samara. Uruguay won their three games so both they and Russia advanced to the knock-out stage. Spain and Portugal played a 3-3 thriller in Sochi, with Ronaldo equalising in the last minute but both teams qualified for the next stage. Croatia defeated Argentina 3-0 and won all three games in their group. Both teams also qualified for the next round.

Elimination of Germany

The only big surprise so far, was the elimination of Germany. They needed a draw against South Korea in their final group game, in Kazan, but South Korea scored two goals in injury time and relegated Germany to bottom position in the group. England and Belgium qualified for the next round, with Belgium leading the group but by finishing runner up, England avoided Brazil, Netherlands, Spain and Argentina in the other half of the draw.

England self-doubt

Russia defeated Spain, in Moscow, in the round of 16, but the hosts were knocked out by Croatia on penalties, in the quarter-finals, in Sochi. England survived a scare against Colombia, in Moscow, but beat Sweden comfortably, in Samara, to arrive in the heady heights of a World Cup semi-final for the first time since 1990. There they met Croatia, in Moscow and after taking the lead with a Trippier free-kick in the fifth minute, they seemed to suffer from complete confusion. "Do we attack and get another goal or do we try to hang on to our lead for the rest of the game." England's performance got steadily worse as the game progressed and they literally handed the match to Croatia, with Modric taking control of midfield and with two lively wingers. It was no surprise when Perisic scored the winning goal in extra-time.

Belgium eliminate Brazil

In the other half of the draw, Belgium succeeded in beating Brazil, in Kazan, then lost to France in Saint Petersburg. France then had an advantage playing in the same Saint Petersburg Stadium in the semi-final against Belgium and managed to win 1-0 so the stage was set for a France v Croatia final with France the firm favourites.

The final

The Luzhniki Stadium in Moscow was the scene of the first ever World Cup final in Russia. The match got off to a great start and both sides had scored by the 18th minute, France with the first own-goal scored in a World Cup final. France then took a stranglehold grip over the game and by the 65th minute were leading 4-1 but their second goal was the subject of some controversy and the hand-ball decision given against Perisic by VAR was hotly disputed. Argentinian referee Nestor Pitana was not involved in the penalty decision but was criticised for awarding the free-kick which led to France's first goal.

Legacy of the Russian World Cup

So, the controversial Russian World Cup was over, their team reached the quarter-finals and each game was well attended with 78,000 people at the final in Moscow. The organisers are to be congratulated for putting together a successful World Cup with very little crowd disturbance. Russia is not ideal for a World Cup with stadiums thousands of miles apart but the teams seem to have handled the travelling between venues without too much upheaval.

French unity

French football fans felt the World Cup win brought some unity to the country after experiencing difficult times over the past 20 years. France is a country embracing many religions and cultures and protests over ever-increasing poverty and unemployment have at times got out of control. The unity fans feel as result of this victory hopefully will help the government find solutions to the many issues that face them.

Watershed moment

Russian sport has suffered following allegations during the period 2014-2016, that their laboratory staff swapped contaminated urine samples with clean ones so that Russian athletes would not fail doping tests. A whistle-blower, who has been named, notified western media of the doping scheme which has led to investigations by the official Global Anti-Doping Agency. This has caused the banning of Russian athletes and sportsmen from participation in major events, including the 2016 Olympic Games in Rio de Janeiro, but FIFA allowed Russia to go ahead with preparations for hosting the World Cup.

Winning coach

Didier Deschamps

As a player he played over 100 times for three different clubs, Nantes, Marseille and Juventus and was part of the victorious French team in the 1998 World Cup on home territory. He also played over 100 times for the French national team as a holding midfielder. If he wins the 2022 World Cup, he will be the third footballer to win as both player and coach, following in the footsteps of Mario Zagallo and Franz Beckenbauer. In 2022 he will be missing, N'golo Kante and Karim Benzema, winner of the 2022 Ballon d'Or. Attention to detail, the ability to manage one or two prima donnas in his squad and get the best out of his players at all times are the qualities that has made him one of the most successful French coaches in history.

2018 World Cup Final

15th July 2018

Luzhniki Stadium, Moscow

France 4 Croatia 2

2014 World Cup

Brazil

"The 7-1 catastrophe for the Brazilians in Belo Horizonte had a devastating effect on football fans all over Brazil"

The home of football

So, the 2014 World Cup returns, according to the Brazilian people, to the real home of football but there might be dissention from the Argentinians and Uruguayans because serious international football started not in Brazil, nor in the textile factory towns in Manchester and Preston, as English fans might believe, but in the Olympic Games of 1924 and 1928, the first truly international football tournaments, when Uruguay and Argentina reigned supreme.

Withdrawal of Colombia

Brazil had been a regular bidder for the World Cup since 1978, such is the passion for the game. The only other nation bidding for hosting of the 2014 World Cup was Colombia and they eventually withdrew when the strength of support for Brazil became more apparent. FIFA is also known for not accepting bids from countries with a poor national security record which could stand in the way of future bids by Colombia.

High-scoring tournament

After a history of low scoring in past World Cups, this one looked different. Brazil scored three goals against Croatia in Sao Paulo and then added four more against Cameroon in Brasilia. Croatia then joined the party by also scoring four against Cameroon in Manaus, the first time a World Cup match had been held in Amazonas. Netherlands then beat Spain 5-1 in Salvador and qualified for the knock-out competition with a perfect record. Colombia followed suit in the next group, also winning all three matches including a 4-1 defeat of Japan in Cuiaba, in Mato Grosso, also hosting a World Cup match for the first time.

Costa Rica win tough group

Another surprise was soon forthcoming as, in a group consisting of three World Cup winners, the fourth team, Costa Rica, succeeded in qualifying, defeating Uruguay and Italy in the process. Their progress continued in the knock-out stage and they made it the quarter-finals, where they were finally eliminated on penalties by Netherlands, but by that time, had their most successful tournament in their brief football history. England had a dismal time and were eliminated after two defeats against Italy, in Manaus and Uruguay in Sao Paulo. France were also heavy scorers with five against Switzerland in Salvador and three against Honduras in Porto Alegre.

World Cup final at the Maracanã

Awaiting Germany in the final, as in 1990, were a less-than impressive Argentinian team, who had battled their way into the final with a series of narrow wins. It is worth looking at their results: Nigeria 3-2, Iran 1-0, Bosnia 2-1, Switzerland 1-0, Belgium 1-0 and Netherlands on penalties. It is doubtful whether any team has ever reached the final with less impressive results. However, they made it to the final for the fifth time which is a great record but for the third time they finished on the losing side. They held the heavy-scoring Germany team until extra-time when Götze scored the winner with seven minutes remaining. Germany had succeeded in scoring a total of seventeen goals in the tournament and were worthy winners of their fourth World Cup trophy.

Two-time defeat in front of their fans

Brazil will have memories, not only of their massacre by Germany in Belo Horizonte, but also of their defeat by Uruguay in the 1950 final. This was the second time Brazil had hosted the World Cup and each time their passionate fans had high expectations of success but failed at the finishing line on both occasions.

Watershed moment

The historic Brazil v Germany encounter

In the knock-out stage right up to the semi-finals, matches were won by the finest of margins until the semi-final match between Germany and Brazil in Belo Horizonte, scene of England's defeat by the USA in the 1950 World Cup. As in 1950, no one could have predicted what was about to happen. Brazilian fans turned up in Belo Horizonte with high expectations of a win which would take them to the Maracanã for the final. What they received instead was a defeat of staggering proportions, which set several records. Germany scored five goals in the space of eighteen minutes and added two more in the second half to complete a 7-1 win. There were doubtless many reasons for their capitulation but the most acceptable from the Brazilians fans perspective was that they were playing without Neymar and, more importantly, without Thiago Silva, for many years the backbone of the Brazilian defence. This was Brazil's first competitive home defeat for 39 years and it reduced some Brazilian fans to tears and others to cheering every Germany move. Their coach Luiz Felipe Scolari, has had an amazingly successful career but throughout his retirement, hastened by this match, he will be remembered in Brazil, not for his many triumphs, but for this match, which marked the darkest day in Brazilian football history.

Winning coach

Joachim Loew

Jurgen Klinsmann can be credited with at least partial responsibility for Loew's successful career as Germany's coach as he appointed him as his assistant in

2004. When Klinsmann stepped down in 2006, Loew took over the national team and stayed for the next 15 years, the longest period not only of any German coach but also of any European coach except Vittorio Pozzo of Italy in the 1920s and 1930s. He enjoyed a win ratio of 62% and of 198 games in charge of the national team, he won 124 of them. His success more than anything else was due to his renowned attention to detail and creation of a winning mentality amongst his players.

2014 World Cup Final

13ᵗʰ July, 2014

Maracaña Stadium, Rio de Janeiro

Germany 1 Argentina 0

2010 World Cup

South Africa

"Primera victoria para España "

Africa's turn

South Africa missed out in 2006 but made sure of the 2010 World Cup when FIFA decided that the host country would come from the African continent. Egypt and Morocco, who seem to apply for every World Cup, were the two countries to miss out. At the hosting ceremony, in 2004, 85-year-old Nelson Mandela described how important football was in his life in prison and held up the World Cup for all to see.

Allegations

In 2015, there were media reports that the South African bid committee had secured the votes to stage the finals by paying a bribe of US$10 million to Jack Warner and other FIFA executives. Furthermore, ex-FIFA executive Chuck Blazer, having secured a plea-bargain to cooperate with the FBI, confirmed he and other FIFA executives received bribes to ensure the selection of South Africa as the hosting country and also that Morocco and not South Africa had in fact won the voting to stage the tournament.

Ghana's exciting journey

Six African nations qualified for the finals but only Ghana managed to progress through the group stage. Their team, one of the most entertaining of the tournament, which gained more and more support after each success secured victories over Serbia and the USA. In the quarter final against Uruguay in Johannesburg, in the last minute of extra-time, Luis Suarez stopped a certain goal with his hand on the goal line and with the whole of Africa taking a deep breath, Asomoah Gyan hit the crossbar with his penalty, taking the game to a penalty shoot-out which Ghana were unable to win.

Rob Green error

England made headlines again and a ghastly goalkeeping error by Rob Green did not get them off to a good start against USA at Rustenburg and they had to be satisfied with a 1-1 draw. The error took the wind out of England's sails and sadly, Rob Green didn't play in another match in this tournament but was recalled in 2012 by Roy Hodgson.

Sixteen goals for Germany

England were to hit the headlines again in their round of sixteen match against Germany. Frank Lampard scored a goal which TV replays showed was at least two feet over the line but as in 1986, England were again robbed. Germany, exploiting two weak full backs, were two nil up at the time but England were fighting back and again they could not get over their moment of misfortune and were soundly beaten by the Germans 4-1. Germany in fact scored four goals against Australia in the group game, four against England and another four against Argentina in the quarter-finals, before being defeated by Spain in Durban in the semi-final. Germany had, in fact, scored a total of 16 goals throughout the tournament which included the three goals they scored against Uruguay in the third-place play-off. Thomas Muller was one of the leading goal scorers with a total of five goals.

Six wins for Netherlands not enough to beat Spain

Netherlands had battled their way through to the final in Johannesburg, by virtue of wins against Denmark, Japan, Cameroon, Slovakia, Brazil and Uruguay – six wins which are very rarely achieved in a World Cup, but unfortunately, they were unable to achieve a seventh and went down to a victorious Spanish team who won the World Cup for the first time. A fierce encounter resulted in a 0-0 draw after 90 minutes with Andres Iniesta securing a win for Spain five minutes from time. This was a golden era for Vicente del Bosque and his Spanish team as they followed their World Cup victory by winning the 2012 European Championship in Poland and Ukraine, this time defeating Italy 4-0 in Kyiv.

Watershed moment

No luck for the Irish

Before the World Cup started there was already controversy. In a play-off match for World Cup qualification, France and Ireland played a two-leg match. In the first in Dublin, France managed to win 1-0. In the second leg in Paris, Ireland were leading 1-0, when, in extra-time, Thierry Henry deliberately handled the ball to stop it going out of play. In so doing he knocked the ball on to his other hand so he in fact handled the ball twice. The referee claimed he was unsighted and did not stop play so Henry crossed the ball to William Gallas who scored the goal which put France into the World Cup finals. This had a much more dramatic impact on the game than the Maradona "Hand of God" which was in some parts of the world considered quite clever. Henry's was not clever and it led to several years of social media abuse for the player and the Swedish referee, Martin Hansson. Both player and referee were almost driven into retirement. Attempts by the Irish Football Association to arrange a replay fell on deaf ears.

Winning coach

Vicente del Bosque

The 2010 World Cup winning coach had a highly successful playing career with Real Madrid, playing in more than 500 league and cup matches, winning the

Spanish league on five occasions and the European Cup on two occasions. As Spain's coach he won not only the 2010 World Cup but also the EUFA European Championship in 2012 with virtually the same team. He was one of the very few Spanish footballers who was ennobled by the monarchy, having been created Marquess del Bosque by King Juan Carlos. del Bosque spent an incredible 33 years at Real Madrid as a player and a coach and supervised the development of a number of the World Cup winning players including Iker Casillas, Xabi Alonso and Xavi. One of his biggest challenges was managing the rivalry between Barcelona and Real Madrid players within the squad. Even selecting the Spanish team must, at times, have been highly controversial.

2010 World Cup Final

11th July 2010

Soccer City, Johannesburg

Spain 1 Netherlands 0

2006 World Cup

Germany

"Quarta vittoria per gli Italiani"

No surprises

2006 was a World Cup for the favourites and leading teams and all four semi-finalists were from Europe. Of the smaller countries only Ukraine and Portugal had good campaigns and reached the quarter-finals with Argentina and Brazil also being eliminated in the quarter-finals. Angola, Ghana, Trinidad and Tobago and Togo were making their first appearances but none of them progressed from their groups.

England fail in the penalty shoot-out once more

England breezed through their group and beat Ecuador in the round of sixteen before meeting one their nemeses, Portugal in the quarter-finals at Gelsenkirchen. Rooney had been sent off in the 62nd minute but England held on into extra-time before Lampard, Gerrard and Carragher all missed penalties in the shoot-out and Ronaldo, who had a hand in Rooney's sending off, despatched the winning penalty and England were on the way home once again.

The final goes to another penalty shoot-out

The final between Italy and France at the Olympic Stadium, Berlin, featured numerous legends of the game with Italy fielding Buffon, Cannavaro, Gattuso, Pirlo and Totti and France, Barthez, Thuram, Vieira, Zidane and Henry. It was beautiful to watch but the teams only managed one goal apiece with Italy winning the penalty shoot-out with five perfect penalties.

Italy's fourth win

This was Italy's fourth World Cup win and they are one of the teams like Germany and Brazil, who have the ability to play under pressure and close off vital games. It will not be the last time that these teams feature in the last rounds of a World Cup tournament but, sadly for them, Italy failed to qualify for the 2022 World Cup and will therefore not feature in Qatar.

Watershed moment

Zidane's headbutt

As the World Cup Final was entering its final moments, Zinedine Zidane and Marco Materazzi, who had been tussling from the start of the match, said something to each other, upon which Zidane turned round and headbutted Materazzi in the middle of his chest. Italian players who had witnessed the incident surrounded Argentinian referee Horacio Elizondo, who was unsighted and all he saw was Materazzi lying on the ground. Initially, it looked like Zidane was going to escape punishment, then referee Elizondo went to the fourth official who confirmed the foul. Zidane was dismissed and that was the unfortunate end of his World Cup career as he announced his retirement immediately after the match. Zidane would have been one of France's penalty-takers and his influence could have changed the result. A moment of pure madness. Materazzi, years later, indicated that after many unpleasant exchanges between the two, Zidane had offered to give him his shirt after the game, whereupon Materazzi had responded "I'd prefer your sister." Zidane has wisely remained silent on the matter.

Winning coach

Marcello Lippi

Highly respected coach who has managed Juventus, Napoli and Inter Milan. Successful coaches have a number of essential skills – to be able to manage the prima donnas in the team, to be able to handle pressure, to recover quickly for adversity and most of all to keep the team motivated and enthusiastic all the time. Lippi is high on list of all-time great coaches.

2006 World Cup Final

9th July 2006

Olympiastadion, Berlin

Italy 1 France 1

(Italy win 5-3 on penalties)

2002 World Cup

South Korea and Japan

"Fifth win for the Brazilians in Yokohama"

Joint bid

The joint bid of South Korea and Japan was agreed in 1996, giving them six years to prepare for the event, a little more than Uruguay were given in the first World Cup finals in 1930, when the hosts, Uruguay, were given just twelve months to prepare for the event which included building a new stadium for the final. How times have changed with the World Cup now being recognised as the most prestigious sporting event in the world. There were many nations in 1930, who disagreed with the concept of establishing a tournament involving European and South American teams due to the necessity for a twenty-day sea voyage either way but Jules Rimet, faced with fierce opposition, managed to persevere with his dream and much credit must go to him for navigating his way through many logistics issues of that era.

The 2002 tournament final was to be played in Japan at the International Stadium in Yokohama and FIFA welcomed China, Ecuador, Senegal, and Slovenia who were making their first appearance in the World Cup finals.

France eliminated without scoring a goal

The first shock of the tournament was caused by the holders of the World Cup, who failed to score a single goal in being eliminated in the group stage, the first time such a calamity had hit the holders of any World Cup. It is very likely that their abject performance was caused by the fact that they qualified automatically and did not have the benefit of regular competitive football over the previous year. France were eliminated by virtue of defeats by Senegal and Denmark with Thierry Henri being sent off in the Uruguay match, maybe because of frustration with his team's performance.

England v Argentina yet again

England faced Argentina for the fourth time since 1966 with David Beckham gaining retribution for his sending off in 1998 by despatching a penalty which not only won the match for England but also helped eliminate Argentina from the tournament. Playing in the Argentinian team was Mauricio Pochettino, ex-Spurs and PSG manager together with Diego Simeone, currently manager of Atletico Madrid – not a midfield to be messed with.

South Korea's best performance

South Korea had an amazing tournament defeating Portugal, Italy and Spain, three of the most successful European teams and reached the semi-finals before losing 1-0 to Germany who reached their fifth final. However, the most successful team at the tournament, Brazil, eased their way through the field and reached their seventh final, in a dream match against the second most successful World Cup team, Germany.

England v Brazil

The USA had their most successful tournament to date defeating both Portugal and Mexico before being narrowly beaten by Germany in the quarter finals. England, after defeating Denmark 3-0 in the Round of 16, met their nemesis, Brazil, who they had never defeated in a competitive tournament. Watching a Brazilian team containing Ronaldinho, Ronaldo, Rivaldo, Roberto Carlos and Cafu would be excellent entertainment but you wouldn't want to play against them and that is exactly what England had to do and they in fact took the lead in the first half through Michael Owen. Rivaldo equalised and Ronaldinho then scored what turned out to be the winner with a lobbed freekick over the head of David Seaman. Then England had that little bit of luck missing in games such as these, when Ronaldinho was sent off by Mexican referee Felipe Ramos Rizo. However, when they needed strength and determination, all we saw was a tired England team with no idea how to break down the Brazilian defence for the equaliser so, not for the first time before the semi-final stage, England were on their way home.

Two most successful World Cup teams meet in final

Yokohama staged the final between Brazil and Germany and by the time of the final, Brazil had already acquired a semblance of invincibility. They again played inspiring football and two goals from Ronaldo in the second half were enough to defeat the Germans, who, like England before them, had developed a rather haggard look following their seventh game in three weeks. This was Brazil's fifth win in the World Cup and if there was any doubt before, they have now clearly established themselves as the most successful team in World Cup history and will certainly start the 2006 World Cup to be held in Germany, as tournament favourites.

Watershed moment

Ireland made it through their group before going out to Spain on penalties but not before they were the subject of an incredible bust-up between their captain and most experienced player, Roy Keane and Mick McCarthy, the Ireland manager. At a team meeting, after McCarthy had criticised Keane's behaviour, Keane unleashed a torrent of abuse against McCarthy which led to McCarthy having no option but to send Keane home. The team meeting featured a heated debate on the playing conditions of the training facility given to Ireland on the Pacific Island of Saipan.

Winning coach

Luis Felipe Scolari

"Big Phil' as he was known when he joined Chelsea, successfully managed one of the all-time great Brazilian teams to victory in Yokohama. With legendary players, Cafu, Roberto Carlos, Rivaldo, Ronaldinho and Ronaldo they were virtually unbeatable and even in the quarter-final, when down to ten men for half the game, they managed to hold on and beat England. His career with Chelsea was a short one as his English was not fluent and frankly he didn't have the same players at his disposal. A great character, he also had success with Portugal in the European Championship.

2002 World Cup Final

30th June 2002

International Stadium, Yokahama

Brazil 2 Germany 0

1998 World Cup

France

"La France pour la première fois"

The Brazil doctor said later *"Imagine if I had refused to allow Ronaldo to play and Brazil lost, I would have had to hide somewhere."*

France hosts for first time since 1938

The only other country competing to host the 1998 World Cup was Morocco and FIFA were not ready to host the event in the Middle East. This was second time France had been chosen as the host country following the 1938 final, played shortly before the outbreak of war.

No luck for the Scots

Uruguay, Portugal, Czech Republic and Russia failed to qualify and Croatia, Jamaica, Japan and South Africa were making their first appearance. In Group A Scotland were defeated 3-0 by Morocco and failed to qualify for the next round for the eighth time. France and Argentina were the only countries to win all their games and progressed to the knock-out stage. Spain defeated 1994 heroes, Bulgaria, 6-1 but were knocked out by Nigeria.

England v Argentina

England, by virtue of two good wins against Colombia and Tunisia, were drawn to play against their bête noir,

Argentina, and the match at St Etienne's stadium was one of the most entertaining of the tournament. Two early penalties for each side started things off and then 18-year-old Michael Owen, only playing because of media pressure on manager Glenn Hoddle, scored a superb goal which helped launch Owen's career. He took the ball from the half-way line, swerved past two defenders and before scoring a goal to remember to put England into the lead, but two disasters hit England over the next hour. Firstly, David Beckham was given a red card by Danish referee, Kim Milton Nielsen. Then came the penalties and Paul Ince and David Batty failed to score, leaving England, not for the first or last time, on the losing side in a penalty shoot-out. Batty, as the media reminded us, had never taken a penalty kick before in a football league match. So, as in 1990, England found the penalty shoot-out too much for them.

The final everyone wanted France v Brazil

France needed penalties to beat Italy at Saint-Denis and reached the final for the first time. Brazil defeated Chile 4-1, Denmark 3-2 and needed penalties against Netherlands in Marseille but managed to reach their sixth final at Saint-Denis.

Watershed moment

Ronaldo – in or out

Ronaldo, Brazil's leading player, suffered a convulsive fit hours before the game and was not in the starting line-up. Coach Mario Zagallo, winner of the 1970 World Cup, then feared an unfavourable reaction if he didn't play Ronaldo so the team was changed. Ronaldo, however, was still feeling the effects of his seizure and his presence seemed to unsettle his team and France won the match 3-0, thanks to two headed goals by Zidane.

Winning coach

Aimé Jacquet

After enjoying a lengthy playing career with Saint-Etienne and Lyon, Jacquet had successful management spells at Lyon and Bordeaux and was later appointed assistant to national team manager Gerard Houllier. He took over as acting coach of the national team in 1994, but was never popular and the media was always trying to remove him. All went well in the World Cup, however, played on home turf and their performances improved as the tournament progressed, finally ending successfully, as France won the World Cup for the very first time after 68 years of failure, their first appearance having been in the 1930 World Cup.

1998 World Cup Final

12th July, 1998

Stade de France, Paris

France 3 Brazil 0

1994 World Cup

USA

"World Cup arrives at the Land of the Brave"

This is an article I wrote describing the 1930 World Cup - *"With the USA experiencing such a surge of interest in soccer, the 1930 World Cup was a timely opportunity for showcasing their remarkable progress and the USA team was one of the successes of the tournament."*

The World Cup comes home

The USA qualified for the World Cup in 1934, but were defeated in the first round. The next time they qualified was in 1950 when they achieved a sensational win against the England team, who were at that time amongst the favourites for the tournament. They wouldn't have known it in 1950, but the USA national team would not qualify for another World Cup for 40 years until the 1990 tournament in Italy, followed, of course, in 1994, by the biggest event in American soccer history, when the World Cup literally came home, to the "Land of the Brave."

Stadiums all in place

Yes, in 1994, the World Cup came to the USA for the very first time and the excitement it created was quite immense. Due to the incredible success and popularity of American Football all over the USA in the past 70 years, they had the best stadiums in the world, most of them holding a minimum of 80,000 people, all ready for immediate use and this was the key element in the bidding process to host the event as the stadiums in the other competing countries were either found to be deficient or required the building of new stadiums. The USA only had one objective – to make their World Cup the biggest and the best and nothing was going to stand in their way. At the time of their bid, the USA had no recognised national professional football league and FIFA insisted that they create one. Major League Soccer was therefore established in 1993 and it still remains intact today.

Jim Brown, one of heroes of 1930 World Cup

As part of the opening ceremony at Soldier Field stadium in Chicago, the home of the Chicago Bears, one of the heroes of the 1930 World Cup, 84-year-old Jim Brown, was wheeled onto the field in a wheelchair to meet World Cup dignitaries to a tumultuous welcome. Jim's son, George Brown, also played for the USA national team and both are in the USA's Soccer Hall of Fame. Jim Brown was later signed by Manchester United and played over 40 games for them before moving to Brentford and Spurs. Sadly, Jim died four months after his great welcome at Soldier Field.

Debutants and rule changes

Greece, Nigeria and Saudi Arabia were appearing for the first time, Russia appeared as a separate nation for the first time, following the breakup of the Soviet Union, and for the first time since 1938, a unified Germany took part in the tournament. Also, for the very first time the World Cup was decided by penalties. Other changes introduced by FIFA to encourage attacking play were an increase in number of points for a win to three points and a ban on back passes to the goalkeeper with the foot.

Successful tournament by Bulgaria

The shock result of the tournament was the defeat of Germany, the reigning champions, by Bulgaria, who went on to reach the semi-final. Their legendary striker, Hristo Stoichkov, who played over 200 games for Barcelona, was the joint-leading scorer of the tournament, in which Bulgaria had defeated Argentina, Greece, Mexico and Germany before losing to Italy 2-1 in the semi-final. This was by far the best performance in their World Cup history but their qualification for the 1998 World Cup in France was the last time Bulgaria would be seen in the World Cup. One of the best individual performances was by Russian striker, Oleg Salenko, who scored five goals in a 6-1 defeat of Cameroon at Stanford Stadium, although his team were unable to progress to the knock-out stage. This remains the highest number of goals scored by a player in a World Cup match.

USA qualifies for knock-out stage

The United States qualified from a tough group, after defeating Colombia in that infamous match at the Rose

Bowl and drawing with Switzerland at the Pontiac
Silverdome but in the match all their fans dreamed of,
they were defeated 1-0 by Brazil at Stanford University
Stadium on 4th July. Brazil went on to defeat
the Netherlands in the quarter-final and Sweden in the
semi-final to reach their fifth final.

Ireland's shock win against Italy

Ireland had created a sensation in their group by
defeating Italy with a famous goal by Ray Houghton at
the Giants Stadium but the Italians made it through to the
knock-out stage with a narrow win against Norway and a
draw against Mexico followed by an extra-time win
against Nigeria in the next round.

The final

Italy v Brazil at the Rose Bowl in front of 94,000 ecstatic
fans - stuff to dream of but disappointing as the match
produced no goals at all and finally after 120 minutes of
near misses and solid defensive play from both teams –
never giving an inch – the dreaded penalty shoot-out
arrived for which no team is ever prepared. Brazil led
after four rounds with one miss each and Baggio had to
score to keep Italy in the match. Unfortunately, he joined
the ever-increasing list of players missing penalties in a
World Cup as Baggio's shot went high over the bar, a
product of stress and the magnitude of the occasion. So,
Brazil proved triumphant for the fourth time after wins
in 1958, 1962, 1970 and now in 1994.

Win dedicated to Ayrton Senna

Brazilian fans dedicated their win to Formula One driver, Ayrton Senna, who had died in an accident at the San Marino Grand Prix just two months before the final.

Watershed moment

Andres Escobar tragedy

Colombia was the feature of a tragic event. Andres Escobar, one of their team's defenders was shot dead in Medellin, a few days after the World Cup, after scoring an own goal in the match against the USA at the Rose Bowl, which contributed to the elimination of Colombia from the competition. Betting syndicates and drugs cartels were a heavy influence in Colombian football at that time but this tragedy cast a shadow over international football for some time.

Winning coach

Carlos Alberto Parreira

Unlike the other famous Carlos Alberto, Parreira was not a player but as a coach he holds a record that might never be beaten, together with Bora Milutinovic, who, coincidentally, was the USA's coach at the 1994 World Cup. Both have taken five teams to the World Cup, in Parreira's case, Kuwait, the UAE, Saudi Arabia, Brazil and South Africa. It was always said that the easiest job in the world was being coach to a Brazilian team because the players themselves are so creative and disciplined. They live and breathe football and never stop practicing. Parreira's coaching career spanned 40 years and he coached teams all over the world.

1994 World Cup Final

17th July 1994

Rose Bowl, Pasadena

Brazil 0 Italy 0

(Brazil win 3-2 on penalties)

1990 World Cup

Italy

"German domination once more"

Maradona at the end of his tether

There was a feeling before the 1990 World Cup Final started that the behaviour of the Argentinians during the World Cup was so disgraceful that there was no way that any referee was going to allow them to win a third trophy, and so it proved. Time and time again in the final Maradona ran into tackles and sprawled onto the ground in hope or was it despair? It was so tragic that the career of a player so talented should end like this. Other teams had worked so hard for their loyal fans and would have given anything for a place in the World Cup Final but somehow Argentina thought there was a short cut to winning the World Cup, without the hard work, just focussing on free-kicks, penalties and maybe red cards. Compared to the Mario Kempes team of 1978 and the Maradona team of 1986 (despite the "hand of God" incident), this 1990 team was an utter shambles and how they made it to the final, scoring just five goals in six games and helped by two penalty shoot-outs, defies belief.

The hosting enigma

The host country for the 1990 World Cup was eventually whittled down to England Greece, Soviet Union and Italy, this being the first of nine attempts by England to stage the World Cup again.

England's almighty effort

In a tournament marked by sixteen red cards, four penalty shoot-outs, eight extra-times and low scoring throughout, England proved no exception, after escaping from a group in which only seven goals were scored, their 1-0 win over Egypt being the only win of the six matches. They then defeated Belgium with a superlative effort from David Platt then played a breath-taking match against everyone's favourite second team, Cameroon, in the quarter-final and after going behind 2-1 they eventually overcame the impressive Africans 4-2. Star player, 38-year-old Roger Milla, delighted the fans not only with his superb goals but also with his entertaining goal celebrations. Reaching the heady heights of the semi-final for the first time in 24 years, England now faced the mighty West Germans for the last time, their country dropping the "West" following re-unification with East Germany in 1992.

Schillaci!

An Italian hero was also emerging in Salvatore Schillaci, who after scoring as a substitute against Austria in the group games, became a regular fixture in the Italian team and would finish as the tournament's leading scorer. Italy won all its group games by small margins, in keeping with the rest of the tournament, although Czechoslovakia did manage to break the mould by defeating the USA 5-1. In another group, the United Arab Emirates, reaching the World Cup for the first time, were defeated 5-1 by West Germany and 4-1 by Yugoslavia.

Drawing of lots

In England's group, there was another first, this time the drawing of lots to decide 2nd and 3rd place in the group between Ireland and Netherlands, who had identical records, which Ireland won. The possibility of lots has now been removed from future competitions. In most groups three teams qualified, one of the exceptions being Andy Roxburg's Scotland, who, for the fourth time in a row, were catching an early flight home.

Stumbling Argentina

Argentina defeated a below-par Brazilian team in the round of 16, and proceeded to the final by virtual of a 1-0 win, penalties against Yugoslavia in the quarters and Italy on penalties in the semi-final. By this time absolutely no one except ardent Argentinian fans were supporting this team which just stumbled from one win to the next. Ireland succumbed to Italy after an impressive tournament.

England v Germany, not for the first time

So, to Turin for the much-awaited England v Germany semi-final. It was England's biggest chance of a final since 1970 when they yielded a 2-0 lead in the historic game on a hot summer's day in Leon. England had match winners in Lineker, Gascoigne, Platt, Beardsley, Barnes and Waddle but in keeping with the rest of the tournament goals proved difficult and an early own goal by Germany was wiped out by a late Lineker strike, taking the game into the eighth extra-time of the tournament and thence into a disastrous penalty shoot-out.

World Cup final, Estadio Olimpico, Rome

England were knocked out on penalties for the first of many times, Germany marched to their third final and they had the benefit of knowing that no referee was going to allow the Argentinians to win this World Cup. So, it proved, Germany won the title with a penalty, hotly disputed by the Argentinians, of course, who spent most of the game, either flailing on the ground or surrounding Brazilian referee, Jose Ramiz Wright, who became a legend in Brazil after sending off five players in a Copa Libertadores match in 1981. Well, he added two more to his collection at Rome's Estadio Olimpico, on 8th July, 1990, by sending off Argentina's Pedro Monzon, the first red card in a World Cup Final and also Gustavo Dezotti, in a quite shameful exhibition of football with Argentina ending the tournament with just nine players.

Maradona's contribution to Argentinian football

From 1966 at Wembley Stadium, when Antonio Rattin was sent off and Alf Ramsey called them "animals," to 1990, in Rome, nothing seems to have changed in Argentinian football except the emergence of one of the greatest players in the history of the game. Maradona tried for a period to raise the credibility of Argentinian football round the world, and for a short period he succeeded but his contribution in 1990 did nothing to enhance his public image. Let us hope for better things in the USA in 1994.

Lionel Messi's breath of fresh air

Thankfully, Lionel Messi, with his incredible artistry, has repaired a lot of the damage done to Argentinian football and his professional approach to the game has been a breath of fresh air to Argentinian football.

Watershed moment

Penalties, not for the first time

It has been proven many times that however much you prepare for penalties, you cannot practice the stress players must feel in the moment of truth, and sure enough in that moment, Stuart Pearce decided to go straight down the middle and his shot cannoned off goalkeeper Illgner's legs leaving Chris Waddle to keep

England in the tournament. Waddle's is the easiest to remember as it went high into the sky, bounced on to the athletics track and into the safe hands of a spectator. Hopefully, with the benefit of pub humour, Chris Waddle has now got over that one and it has probably turned into one of the England squad's best jokes.

Winning coach

Franz Beckenbauer

Celebrated player who first played in the 1970 World Cup in Mexico at the age of 21. He scored an important goal for West Germany which helped eliminate England in the quarter-final and were then defeated by Italy in the semi-final but went on to win the World Cup in 1974. Together with Mario Zagallo, he is the only footballer who has won the World Cup as a player and coach. He had an illustrious career with Bayern Munich and won the European Cup in three successive seasons from 1974 to 1976, following which he played alongside Pelé for the New York Cosmos from 1977 to 1980. As coach of the national team his only two World Cups were in 1986 and 1990 finishing as runner-up in 1986 and winning the trophy in 1990.

1990 World Cup Final

8th July 1990

Stadio Olimpico, Rome

West Germany 1 Argentina 0

1986 World Cup

Mexico

"With Maradona's two goals, England team had suffered, in the space of four minutes, a double-whammy of historic proportions."

Legendary status

This was Diego Maradona's World Cup and when his life story is written, it sometimes seems that his stardom is limited to the 1986 World Cup, but there is a lot more to his footballing career. Later, at Napoli, he was an absolute legend, adored by the fans and he won two Serie A league titles with them. Ironically, since then Napoli followed Maradona on a downward spiral. The club fell into bankruptcy and Maradona's life suffered a severe decline, but not before he had given incredible entertainment to fans all over the world with his unique ball-playing skills. In 1990, FIFA finally recognised him, along with Pelé, as the greatest footballer of the 20th century. Napoli's fortunes have recently suffered a resurgence and in the 2022/23 season they won Serie A, under coach Luciano Spalletti, by 16 points.

Early years

Diego Maradona was born in 1960 in a suburb of Buenos Aires, one of a family of eight children. The highlight of his early life was taking his youth team Los Cebollitas on an unbeaten run of 136 games. His talent quickly took him to Barcelona at the age of 21 and within two years moved again to Napoli, where he was to become a legend. By that time, he had already demonstrated his skill in the 1982 World Cup, but it was in Mexico, now captain of his team, for which he became best known.

Selection of Mexico

The selection of Mexico as the host country was not achieved without dispute. Colombia had originally been chosen but they pulled out for financial reasons in 1982. There then followed an adverse reaction by the USA and Canada when Mexico was selected. Joao Havelange, the FIFA President had business interests in Mexico and the two countries claimed there was a conflict of interest. Notwithstanding, Mexico's bid went ahead.

England v Argentina, not for the last time

When the claims had been resolved, for the second time in sixteen years, Mexico became the host country. Argentina qualified from the South American group, along with Brazil, Paraguay and Uruguay. They cruised out of the group stage and then met England in the quarter-finals at the Azteca Stadium in Mexico City on 22nd June, 1986.

The "Hand of God"

After an uneventful first half, in the 51st minute an incident occurred which was going to be the talking point of this World Cup and in social media ever since.

A misdirected clearance looped towards England's goal and Shilton jumped for the ball at the same time as Maradona. Shilton is six foot tall with a long reach. Maradona was five foot six inches tall and the only way he could reach the ball was by hand and he miraculously directed the ball into the goal with his left hand. That was fine assuming the referee had a clear view of the occurrence. Yellow card perhaps and free kick to England but Tunisian referee, Ali Bin Nasser was unsighted and as Maradona and his team were celebrating, he saw no reason to disallow the goal.

Fear of reprisals

It was surely the biggest travesty of justice of all time with the referee, due to his inexperience, clearly preferring to award the goal rather than having to deal with the wrath of the Argentinian players. The linesman, with similar lack of experience at this level, also in fear of reprisals from the excitable Argentinians. Casting even further doubt over how this particular incident was allowed to happen, it begs the question why such inexperienced officials were chosen for this major fixture. Neither referee nor linesman was to officiate at this level again.

"Goal of the Century"

The "Hand of God" was followed four minutes later by the "Goal of the Century," which was timed perfectly for many of his fans as it conveniently redeemed Maradona for his role in the "Hand of God" goal. When accused of deception, the easy answer is "but what a goal followed!" The quite sensational goal came as a hammer blow to the England team, still in shock at the previous goal. Maradona seemed to sweep through the whole England defence with Beardsley, Reid, Butcher and Fenwick in the chasing pack, none of them daring to launch a tackle which might earn a caution or worse, finally rounding Shilton and scoring a miraculous goal.

Double-whammy

The goal was celebrated all over the world as one of the greatest on the World Cup stage. The England team had suffered, in the space of four minutes, a "double-whammy" of historic proportions, and to put it mildly, must have been absolutely stunned. How they managed to stop Argentina scoring again must have been another historic feat, but the magic of Maradona shone through this whole World Cup and in most of the games, he was unstoppable so, as in almost every World Cup to date, with the possible exception of 1954, the best team were victorious.

Hindsight

With the benefit of hindsight, after viewing the video clip, a slide tackle by any of the defenders could have ended his run. Maradona said later that he was surprised none of the England players attempted to bring him down and that any other team would have made sure he didn't get past the half way line. He described the England defence as "noble" and credited them with assisting in his brilliant goal. Suddenly, out of the blue, England were 2-0 down although Lineker managed to score before the end.

1986 World Cup winners

Argentina successfully made their way to the final and in an exciting game against Germany, Barruchaga scored the winning goal seven minutes from time so the 1986 World Cup, with all its excitement, went to Argentina for the second time in eight years. After their domination of world football with Uruguay, in 1928 and 1930, they were once again one of the leading footballing nations and for the next 36 years, although they didn't win again, they were always one of the most difficult teams to beat.

Sad end

Maradona continued to shine for club and country but after seven years with Napoli, it was clear he could not handle his celebrity status, and he succumbed like other legends before him, Best and Garrincha, in particular, to a life addicted to drugs and alcohol which contributed to his death in 2020.

Epitaph

In later years, he took on several managerial positions including manager of the Argentinian national team, during which time he was interviewed on Scottish TV on the eve of an Argentina v Scotland match and was asked about the "Hand of God" goal. He said it was a pay-back for England following the Falkland Islands war and the many Argentinian lives lost, Rattin's sending-off in 1966 and England's "lucky" goal against Germany. If nothing else, it showed the resentment there has always been between the two teams which still exists today. Fortunately, he did not blame the 1976 Argentinian revolution on England.

Watershed moment

Refereeing chaos

Probably one of the most discussed incidents in World Cup history, Maradona's hand-ball provoked considerable debate and was clearly seen differently in the two camps. In the Argentinian camp, a triumph of deception, maybe as retribution for other incidents between the two teams. In the England camp it contributed to the team's failure yet again to get past the quarter-finals of a World Cup so the incident stood as an excuse for their elimination. In reality, Argentina were the better team and with Maradona at his peak, they would probably have won the match anyhow. The key to Maradona's deception was in his flamboyant celebration. Urging his team-mates to embrace him, he completely deceived the inexperienced Tunisian referee. After a quick glance at the Bulgarian linesman, Bogdan Dochev, who seemed stunned into indecision, the referee awarded the goal. Dochev spent the rest of his life a virtual recluse as his notoriety was felt to bring shame on his country, post-match video clips clearly showing that it was a handball and as the referee had claimed he was unsighted, the only resource available to correct the referee's decision was Dochev. He admitted later that he saw Maradona handle the ball but claimed the referee did not consult him. This incident should have served as a catalyst for a video review system but another similar incident happened in 2010 in South Africa, when a Frank Lampard shot was filmed two feet over the line.

Winning coach

Carlos Bilardo

Bilardo, who coached Argentina to two successive World Cup Finals, winning in 1986 but failing in 1990 with a style of football which earned universal criticism. In both matches Maradona was the key and he built his 1986 team around this remarkable player but by 1990 Maradona was a shadow of his former self and his lack of energy caused him to stumble into tackles, and he spent most of the match on the ground claiming free-kicks. Bilardo, nonetheless, achieved considerable fame for the two performances.

1986 World Cup Final

29th June 1986

Estadio Azteca, Mexico City

Argentina 3 West Germany 2

1982 World Cup

Spain

"Paolo Rossi returns with a vengeance"

The Falklands War

The Falklands War took place between April and June 1982, hostilities between Argentina and the UK ending six weeks before the World Cup, and despite the fact that there were 900 military casualties in the brief war (most of them Argentinian), there were no serious repercussions, and the two countries avoided each other in the group draws. Both Argentina and England qualified from the group stage, but were then eliminated in the play-off group. Scotland were sent home early following their group matches but Northern Ireland, with 17-year-old Norman Whiteside, managed to win their group and progress to the next round.

Scandals again

Netherlands, World Cup finalists in 1974 and 1978, together with Mexico and Sweden, all failed to qualify for the 1982 World Cup and Algeria, Cameroon, Honduras, Kuwait and New Zealand were all competing for the first time. Italy were slow to start and drew all their group games, qualifying for the next round from Cameroon only on goals scored. The Italian squad were maybe still having difficulty shaking off the after-effects of the Serie A match-fixing scandal.

Three major scandals took place in Gijon, Valladolid and Seville. In Gijon, Germany and Algeria, despite abuse from their fans, played out a 1-0 win for Germany which enabled both teams to qualify for the next round, clearly pre-arranged. An investigation took place and the result was allowed to stand.

El Salvador civil war

In another match at Elche Stadium, Hungary defeated El Salvador, appearing in the World Cup finals for the first time, by 10-1 but the result was not the only disaster the Central American country had been experiencing as they were in the middle of a civil war which was tearing the country apart and which raged from 1979 to 1992.

Another refereeing incident

An incident took place in the semi-final between France and Germany, in Seville. Dutch referee Charles Corver was unsighted when German goalkeeper, Harald Schumacher, blatantly fouled French midfielder Patrick Battiston by twisting round and hitting him in the face with his hip inflicting on the player a broken jaw and damaged vertebrae. Battiston needed oxygen and took no further part in the game. Germany scored two goals against the ten men and reached the World Cup final in a penalty shoot-out. The referee received no assistance from the linesman in this particular case and, of course, in 1982 there was no VAR or fourth official.

Good start by England

Things were looking good for England when in their opening match against France, Bryan Robson scored in the second minute of the game leading to a 3-1 victory but having won their group and progressed to the next group with Spain and Germany they failed to beat either and were eliminated by Germany. So, England went home undefeated but very disappointed with their two 0-0 draws against Germany and Spain. Argentina fielded a 21-year-old Diego Maradona but lost to Italy and Brazil in their group and were eliminated, with Maradona leaving his mark on the World Cup by earning a red card for aiming a kick at a Brazilian defender.

Brazil v Italy

The match of the tournament took place at the Sarria Stadium in Barcelona between Brazil and Italy. Paolo Rossi's hat trick is one of the best remembered in the history of the World Cup, almost matching Geoff Hurst's hat trick in the 1966 final, but Rossi's of course did not win the tournament but it did succeed in eliminating by far the most dangerous team. Brazil had been the stars of the tournament and even in this match played some brilliant football but a vital mistake by Cerezo changed the game and Rossi did the rest.

First penalty shoot-out

Germany beat France in the first penalty shoot-out of the
World Cup in Seville after a pulsating match in which
Germany came back from a 3-1 deficit to tie the match
3-3, which resulted in an Italy v Germany final, played at
the Santiago Bernabeu stadium in Madrid in front of
90,000 fans. Italy won the match 3-1 to complete their
third World Cup Final win. Hero of the tournament was
Paolo Rossi, who had just completed two years in jail for
his role in a match-fixing scandal. He won the Golden
Boot award for being the top scorer in the tournament
and also the Golden Ball award for being the best player
of the tournament. He had certainly earned full
retribution for his crimes.

Watershed moment

*As in Argentina in 1978, there was a political
background to this World Cup. The Falklands War took
place between April and June 1982 and if it hadn't
ended before the World Cup there was a possibility of
England, Scotland and Northern Ireland bowing to
Government pressure to pull out of a tournament in
which their adversary in the war, i.e., Argentina was
playing. This could have had dire consequences for the
World Cup as other allies of Britain could also have
pulled out.*

Winning coach

Enzo Bearzot

Italy's coach for the national and youth teams for 17 years, Bearzot reached the pinnacle of his career by winning the 1982 World Cup but not without some nervous moments. In the group stage, Italy drew all three matches against mediocre opposition in Poland, Peru and Cameroon and then only qualified for the next stage by virtue of scoring one more goal than Cameroon. Italy overcame the favourites, Brazil, in the quarter-finals, with a hat-trick by Paulo Rossi, in a pulsating match which has become one of the world's most featured YouTube matches. Together with Vittorio Pozzo, Bearzot was probably Italy's most renowned coach.

1982 World Cup Final

11th July 1982

Santiago Bernabéu, Madrid

Italy 3 West Germany 1

1978 World Cup

Argentina

"Looking back on this despicable period in Argentinian history, it was indeed remarkable that the 1978 World Cup took place at all."

Finally, it was Argentina's turn

Since their neighbours Uruguay were awarded the 1930 World Cup, Argentina seemed to think they had a right also to host this prestigious event and after missing out in 1950 and 1970, they finally achieved their objective, albeit in political circumstances which had attracted considerable world-wide attention.

The World Cup goes ahead regardless

Of course, when the country was awarded this World Cup back in 1970, there was no sign of the dark years ahead and attempts to remove the hosting from Argentina fell on deaf ears, but looking back on this despicable period in Argentinian history, it was indeed remarkable that the 1978 World Cup took place at all. Some of the players would clearly not feel comfortable about playing in Argentina but of the leading players only Paul Breitner and Johan Cruyff pulled out of their squads on moral grounds or maybe even fear of reprisals.

Controversy yet again

Italy won a tough group consisting of Hungary, France and Argentina and won all three in the process landing Argentina in the next play-off group along with Brazil, which is what they would have wanted to avoid. The fun was just starting in the next round of matches as Argentina and Brazil played out an incredibly tense 0-0 draw in Rosario and after Brazil had beaten Peru 3-0 and Poland 3-1 Argentina found themselves requiring to beat Peru by four goals. They over-did it a bit and by scoring six they surrounded themselves with controversy which has never relented. Allegations of match-fixing by the two teams have never been proven and the result stood so an under-performing Brazil team were eliminated and Argentina moved to their first final since 1930.

Scotland v Netherlands decider

In the final they were to meet an entertaining Netherlands team, aiming to reach the final for the second time in succession, but they had their tricky moments. They scraped through the group stage after failing to beat Peru and then losing to Ally McLeod's Scotland team when two more goals by Scotland, (a hard ask), would have eliminated them. Scotland's downfall was a 3-1 defeat to Peru and failure to beat Iran in Cordoba. As in the last World Cup, they were eliminated on goal difference but only had themselves to blame. A superb individual goal by Archie Gemmell against the Dutch in Mendoza raised the Scots' spirits, and was the highlight of their campaign.

Don Revie scandal

There was turmoil in the England camp since Don Revie resigned from his England post just a year before the World Cup leaving England with a requirement to beat Italy in the final match of their qualifying group to go to Argentina. They failed of course but Revie's resignation attracted wide-scale criticism especially as he had lied about his reasons for missing a South American tour. His acceptance of a financially attractive package as coach to the UAE national team did not make matters any easier for him and he was banned by the Football Association for ten years. Ron Greenwood had taken over the England job but of course failed in his first mission so England failed to qualify for the World Cup for the second year in succession.

Argentina v Netherlands

Having got this far surely the Argentinian team were not going to fail now but the Netherlands had redeemed themselves in the final group matches by defeating Austria 5-1 and Italy 2-1 in a pulsating game in Buenos Aires so the stage was set in the final for two teams that had arguably reached their peak performances in the tournament. In the final, at the Estadio Monumental in Buenos Aires, famous for the ticker-tapes scattered all over the pitch, Mario Kempes' early goal looked like it was going to be decisive but Nanninga equalised with eight minutes left and the game went into extra-time. That was Argentina's moment and the fitter side scored two goals in the last fifteen minutes against an exhausted Netherlands team.

Argentinians celebrate their victory

What the Argentinian victory did for the country is difficult to judge because the "disappearances" didn't stop, with the military government continuing their vicious purge. However, for a while the Argentinian people bathed in the glory of their very first World Cup triumph, to be repeated in eight years' time in Mexico City, where a 25-year-old Diego Maradona showed the world there is more than one way to win a football match.

Watershed moment

1976 Military Revolution

When Jorge Rafael Videla was appointed Head of the Argentinian Army in 1975, he had declared that "people will die in order to make Argentina secure again." Few realised the full significance of his words. In 1976, he replaced Isabel Peron's government with a military junta which, for the next few years, would be responsible for unspeakable crimes, during which thousands of suspected opponents of the government were rounded up, tortured, raped, had their children removed or just "disappeared," The estimated total of "desaparecidos" was anything between 10,000 and 30,000 as no records could be found and the bodies of most of those who disappeared were never recovered. How the 1978 World

Cup was allowed to take place whilst sponsored by this hideous regime is a mystery still defeating logic.

The winning coach

Cesar Luis Menotti

Argentina's coach in the 1978 and 1982 World Cup but with contrasting results as whereas in 1982 his team were defeated three times, in 1978, they actually won the World Cup. He played for his country as a player in the mid-1960s but was not selected in the Argentinian team for the World Cup in England in 1966. One of his sayings was "We have to become of steel and win by any method... obey and function. That's what we expect from the players." His 1978 success earned him an appointment as Barcelona's coach but this World Cup involved too many scandals, despite the star-studded team consisting of players such as Oswaldo Ardiles, Mario Kempes and captain Daniel Passarella, who was soon to follow in Menotti's footsteps and become Argentina's national coach.

1978 World Cup Final

25th June 1978

Estadio Monumental, Buenos Aires

Argentina 3 Netherlands 1

1974 World Cup

West Germany

"First triumph on home territory"

New World Cup trophy

The preparations for the 1974 World Cup in West Germany witnessed one major change – the arrival of a new World Cup an 18-carat gold, 36 cm high trophy which was presented to the West German football authorities in an official ceremony early in 1974. The second change, probably more significant, was the appointment of Joao Havelange from Brazil as the next FIFA President, taking over from Sir Stanley Rous. Havelange was to continue in office for 24 years and then handed over to Sepp Blatter.

1972 Munich Olympic Games tragedy

Security at the 1974 World Cup had been severely strengthened in the light of the tragic events of the 1972 Munich Summer Olympic Games when 11 Israeli coaches and athletes were kidnapped by a Palestinian terrorist group and later died in a botched police raid.

Leading teams failed to qualify

France, Spain and England all failed to qualify for the 1974 World Cup and West Germany welcomed East

Germany for the first time and in fact were drawn together in the same group.

England's frustration at Wembley

England suffered a frustrating time attempting to qualify from a three- team group with Wales and Poland and dropped points against Poland and Wales left England needing to beat Poland in a historic match on 17th October, 1973 at Wembley Stadium. After giving way a goal in the second half and fighting back with an Alan Clarke penalty, they had 30 minutes to score a winning goal which unfortunately never came due to an amazing goalkeeping performance by the Polish goalie, Jan Tomaszewski.

Scotland exit from the World Cup on goal difference

Willy Ormond's Scotland, well equipped with Denis Law, Joe Jordan Billy Bremner and Jimmy Johnstone were drawn in a group with Brazil, Yugoslavia and Zaire who they played in their first match. Two nil up and sailing, Billy Bremner, waved to his players to slow the game down and hold on to their lead. It proved disastrous. The games with the three leading teams were all drawn, Yugoslavia defeated Zaire 9-0 and Brazil needed 3 goals in their game with Zaire which they managed quite easily so Scotland were on the way home, not for the last time and were at that time the only nation to go out of the group stages undefeated. Small consolation.

First match upset

In the first game of the tournament there was a major upset, East Germany defeating West Germany who managed to win their next two games but only finished runner up in their group. However, this proved beneficial as they avoided Brazil, Argentina and Netherlands in the next rounds.

Netherlands "total football" not enough

Rinus Michels "total football" was working well with his Netherlands team and, with the help of the legendary Johan Cruyff, they defeated Argentina and Brazil to reach the final where they met hosts, West Germany. In the final, the first penalty in the history of World Cup Finals was awarded by referee, Jack Taylor, in the Netherland's first attack, in the 2nd minute and a second one to the Germans in the 25th minute. Gerd Muller scored the winning goal in 43rd minute and despite pressure throughout the second half from the talented Dutch side, the Germans held on to win their first of many trophies.

Watershed moment

Sacking of Sir Alf

England's failure to qualify for the 1974 World Cup had tragic consequences. After unimpressive displays by England, in late 1973, following the Poland debacle, the news no one wanted to hear was announced. The Football Association had sacked Sir Alf Ramsey and would commence looking for a replacement. Anyone who had witnessed the amazing performance at Wembley in 1966 must have been totally shell-shocked. Harold Thompson, future Chairman of the Football Association, took it upon himself to do the dirty deed. Thompson was a highly successful man, Oxford degree, later PhD, university lecturer at Oxford who later formed the famous Pegasus football club. However, one member of the FA described him as "a bullying autocrat, a bastard, who treated people like sh…." The biggest problem, however, as far as English football was concerned, was that Thompson did not like Alf Ramsey, who was from humble roots whose one glaring weakness was in the handling of his bosses at the FA so Harold Thompson, now that England had failed to qualify for the 1974 World Cup, had his big opportunity and he took it. Alf Ramsey, suddenly, was no longer in the job he loved and sadly, all he knew was football, and the only people who he respected were his players, and unfortunately, when it was all over, he led a life as a virtual recluse as most of the players he knew best all had their own struggles to survive.

Winning coach

Helmut Schön

Although his name does not immediately spring to mind, Helmut Schön probably had the best record as a national coach than any other. Schön took Germany to the World Cup Final against England in 1966 and to the semi-finals in 1970 when they were defeated 4-3 by Italy. He then won the European Championship in 1972, the World Cup in 1974 and finished runner-up in the European Championship in 1976. Previously as a striker playing for Germany in the late 1930s, he had scored 17 goals in 16 matches.

1974 World Cup Final

7th July 1974

Olympiastadion, Munich

West Germany 2 Netherlands 1

1970 World Cup

Mexico

*"Probably the greatest of all the many successful
Brazilian teams"*

A number of firsts

The first World Cup to be televised world-wide, the
Mexico World Cup was also the best supported of all the
tournaments to date, with crowds exceeding 100,000 for
the final matches and the first to be held in North
America. El Salvador, Israel and Morocco qualified for
the first time. The only other bid to stage the World Cup
was from Argentina and not for the first time their bid
was rejected this time in favour of Mexico's. The 1970
World Cup was to be the first and only time Argentina
have failed to qualify for the event. The El Salvador v
Honduras qualifying match won by the former, triggered
a brief war between the two countries, although the real
causes run deeper and the two countries have historical
disagreements over land reform and immigration.

Scandal in the England camp

Brazil, two time winners were placed in the same group
as World Cup holders England who were the victims of a
mini-scandal when their captain Bobby Moore was
arrested in Colombia for allegedly stealing a bracelet
from a jeweller's shop but he was soon released and

charges were later dropped, when it was discovered that the claimant had made similar allegations in another case involving a celebrity. Having won their first two games Brazil and England met in a group title decider in Guadalajara and in the most entertaining game so far, a goal by Jairsinho decided the match. Both teams went through to the quarter-finals but not before an iconic photo had been taken of Pelé and Bobby Moore exchanging shirts.

Match of the day

In the quarter-final England met West Germany for the first time since the 1966 final in a game which is still talked about today in all the social media platforms. The principal bone of contention from England fans who remember the match is how England managed to lose a 2-0 lead. Excuses start with the "food poisoning" of Gordon Banks the night before the match rendering him incapacitated and unable to take part the next day. This has never been substantiated but as football teams are really careful over their diets and the serving of food in the hotels, it is rather strange that a player should go down with food poisoning a day before a big game. It was clearly quite a serious attack also or Banks would surely have played. His replacement Peter Bonetti was at fault for at least one of the German goals, and has probably never forgotten the match but this was not the only issue. Alf Ramsey has been heavily criticised for substituting Bobby Charlton, despite having failed to score in any of the four games he played in and at the age of 33 was clearly wilting in the 30-degree temperature in Leon. His replacement, Colin Bell, was younger, fitter and was in a better position to defend the lead England still maintained but the debate continues and some fans consider removing Bobby Charlton from the midfield cost England the match. Charlton was also not impressed with his substitution as with his goal tally for England stuck on 49 for ever, he announced his retirement from international football. Conspiracy theories still abound including one that Charlton had been marking Beckenbauer in midfield and when he left the field Beckenbauer had more freedom but Bobby Charlton was always an attacking midfielder or striker and was never used as a defensively. So, for whatever reason, this historic match finished 3-2, probably because Germany were the better team. Germany had their revenge and England not for the first time in the next fifty years were on an early flight home. This was the first time that Germany had beaten England in any match, but not the last!

The final most remembered

Brazil and Italy won their way to the final at the Azteca Stadium, and as it was the first World Cup Final to be televised to a wide audience, it is the final which is best remembered and also for the brilliant play of Pele and his talented team. Goals by Pele, Gerson, Jairsinho and Carlos Alberto clinched the game for Brazil and as it was their third win, they were able to keep the Jules Rimet trophy. Brazil had won all six of their group and knock-out stage matches and also all their qualifying games in their South American group, the first and last time any team has achieved this.

Watershed moment

Charlton's last game

Sadly, the quarter-final game against West Germany proved to be Bobby Charlton's last game for England, after 49 goals in 106 matches, a legend indeed. Bobby had played his first game for England at Hampden Park in April, 1958, two months after the most tragic event in his life when he survived the horrific Munich disaster which took the lives of eight of his team-mates, including his best friend, Duncan Edwards, Roger Byrne, the Manchester United captain and Tommy Taylor, all of whom, almost certainly, would have appeared with him in the 1966 World Cup and maybe even the 1970 World Cup also.

Winning coach

Mario Zagallo

The Brazilian coach, still going strong at the age of 91, had made history, not only with the results but also with the entertainment that his team had provided throughout the tournament for their fans all over the world. Even today, the 1970 World Cup is quoted frequently as being the most entertaining of all finals. The crowning glory was the fourth goal scored by Carlos Alberto. The movement, involved Clodoaldo, who twisted and turned past Mario Bertini, continued by Tostao and ended with Pelé's short pass to the Brazilian right back who thundered the ball past goalkeeper Albertosi. Whether Zagallo had anything to do with the goal or whether it was just conjured up by the superlative skills of his amazing players we shall never know but Zagallo will always take the credit for creating this magical Brazilian team. Zagallo remains, with Franz Beckenbauer, the only footballers who have won the World Cup both as a player and a manage..

1970 World Cup Final

21st June 1970

Estadio Azteca, Mexico City

Brazil 4 Italy 1

Brazilian team which won the 1958 World Cup
front row showing World Cup legends,
Garrincha, Didi, Pelé, Vavá, Zagallo

The Mighty Magyar team of the 1954 World Cup,
unbeaten for 42 matches over a five year period

Italian team after winning the 1938 World Cup in Paris.

The England team that beat West Germany 4-2 in the
1966 World Cup Final

USA team that beat England 1-0 in 1950 World Cup

Bobby Moore and his team celebrate in 1966

1966 World Cup

England

"Alf Ramsey's finest hour"

"………and here comes Hurst. Some people are on the pitch. They think it's all over. It is now. It's four." – Kenneth Wolstenholme

The big day

The mood was ecstatic in London and throughout the UK. The long wait had been arduous and frustrating but here was the national team, on this very day, Saturday, 30th July, 1966, playing in the World Cup Final on the glorious Wembley turf on a bright, sunny day at, of course, 3.00 pm, forty-three years after Billy, the white horse had cleared the way for the for the start of the very first match at Wembley. No horses were necessary this day, no spectators were climbing over the gates, no one dared put a foot on the hallowed Wembley turf and the marching mass bands, marching as though they were going to war, played all the usual football songs, no, not "We will rock you," not even Puccini's "Nessun Dorma," but there was time for the solemn "Abide with me", usually reserved for the Cup Finals.

Poor Jimmy Greaves

The fans sang as though their lives depended on it. All was joy and celebration of this momentous occasion and

all that was left was for those incredible eleven players
to finish it off. There were no substitutes, - they didn't
arrive for World Cup Finals until the next one in 1970 -
so poor Jimmy Greaves had to sit it out on the bench,
fully dressed, now that his injury against France in the
group match was going to keep him out of what would
have been the biggest day of his life. In the end, it was
not so much the injury, as he had recovered, but the fact
there was no one Ramsey could drop to let Greaves back
in, so well had the whole team been playing.

Tickets at turnstiles

I was very fortunate to have tickets for the World Cup
and took my place, standing behind the goal, yes, the one
where Hurst scored his infamous second goal, and I will
say, right now, it was impossible to tell whether the ball
was over the line or not. It just happened in a flash and
then pandemonium. I saw all the matches except the
semi-final, which was played in heavy rain. There were
no ticket touts, no mass buying and selling by agencies
and most of the fans were buying their tickets at the
turnstiles, on the day, at face value, with seating only in
the grandstand and no roof over their heads in most of
the ground. Seats in the stand sold for twenty-five
pounds and a standing room ticket cost three pounds,
seventeen and sixpence. Over one million tickets were
sold for all the games, which of course dwarfed sales for
any previous World Cup.

England's group

England found themselves in a tough group, with
Uruguay, France and Mexico. Uruguay had a history of
success, second to none, and had already won two World
Cups but had lost their way in the last two tournaments.
France had beaten England 5-2 in Paris in 1963 and
finally Mexico, the weakest team in the group, but they
were fighters.

Group of death

England were fortunate, indeed, that they didn't have
Brazil's "group of death," against a Portugal team
containing the brilliant Eusebio, and members of the
Benfica team that were to take on Manchester United in
the European Cup Final in two years' time, including
Torres, Coluna and Simoes. Also drawn in this same
group were 1954 finalists, Hungary and their new star,
Florien Albert. They were not the team of 1954 but still
one of the leading teams in Europe.

The qualification process

What Ramsey and all the experienced coaches
understood full well, of course, and this is true of any
World Cup, was that each team had to go through a
tough qualification process, whether it is in Europe,
South America, Africa, North and Central America or
the Asia and Oceania and only the best teams emerge
victorious from this long, arduous process. So, the teams
that have taken their place in the draw were the best

sixteen in the world, at this point in time. Each team would then go through a rigorous preparation for the tournament ahead of them and by the time of the actual finals, the players would all be fit, motivated and ready for battle.

England's nightmare start

Unfortunately, England did not cruise through the early rounds. They experienced a nightmare of a game against Uruguay, two-time World Cup Champions, who, with their vast experience, knew exactly how to play England, facing their loyal fans for the first time in the tournament, expecting nothing short of a win. Uruguay had figured out that, in order to qualify, they could beat France and Mexico and just needed a draw against England. The Uruguayans played it perfectly. They man-marked England's dangerous players, Charlton Hunt and Greaves who were never able to make an impact on the game. Their tackling was brutal but not dangerous enough to be penalised. The fans became restless. Was this the team that Ramsey said would win the World Cup? The game was played out to a 0-0 draw and the chorus of booing at the end was enough to indicate England had encountered their first crisis but the Uruguayan players were ecstatic. They had achieved what they had set out to do and they were celebrating.

Ramsey survives the second South American challenge

However, Ramsey was certainly not as despondent as the fans. They had endured a tough game against a team that came only to defend and they had survived their first challenge. He had also learned a lot about his team, and still had taken no decision regarding the right- wing position. He had a choice between Connelly, Paine and Callaghan and was to give each of them an opportunity in the group matches. Ramsey had endured, as a player, England's 1-0 defeat to the USA and later the 6-3 battering by Hungary, then watched the sensational 4-2 win over Brazil at Wembley, in 1956. Ramsey was used to the challenge of turning defeat to victory. He knew how difficult the South Americans were and England had at least secured a draw and got over their first game unscathed. As the other group game, France v Mexico game had also ended in a draw, England were back where they started, with two vital games to go which he knew they could win.

Bobby's thunderbolt

Up to the 37th minute in the game against Mexico, England still had not registered their first goal, but a right-footed thunderbolt by Charlton brought a deafening roar from the crowd, and England were back on track, scored once more and found themselves leading the group. A further win against France enabled them to top the group and their worries were over or were they just about to start?

Argentina up next

One team Ramsey wanted to avoid was Argentina and he would have been keeping his eye on their group games with West Germany and Spain, another group of death. However, Argentina failed to beat Germany and found themselves in second position in their group so England were to face their nemesis for the second time in two years and Ramsey will have had memories of that violent encounter and many more that Argentina have experienced since the World Cup started.

History of violence

The behaviour of Luis Monti, San Lorenzo and Argentina centre-half from 1922 till 1930, when he was poached by Juventus, was a determining factor in the decision of British teams to discontinue their visits to the Rio Plata countries culminating in 1929. Southampton had visited Argentina and Uruguay as early as 1904 but the last team to visit was Chelsea in 1929. They had embarked on a three-month tour, which must have been an incredible experience for the players, in a part of the world which was only in its early stage of development but this was the last of the tours for British clubs as Chelsea had returned with negative reports of violence both on the field and amongst its passionate aficionados. Monti is known to have played a significant role in creating Argentina's reputation for unsporting behaviour which included ruthless tackling, headbutting, and referee abuse which often led to crowd violence and pitch invasions. The Chelsea report concluded that it was becoming too dangerous to undertake future tours to the Rio Plata countries, the worst probably being Argentina.

Six players sent off

This was a brief extract from a report of the Celtic v Racing Club of Buenos Aires, for the Intercontinental Cup, at Celtic Park, in October, 1967:- "The Argentinian players tripped, kicked and spat on the Celtic players. When Jimmy Johnstone returned to the dressing room his hair was matted with spit ...." In the return leg in Buenos Aires, Bobby Simpson, the Celtic goalkeeper, was hit by an object thrown by the crowd before the start of the match. As each team had won its home game, a play-off match was arranged in Montevideo and riot police were needed to keep order as the referee lost control and sent off six players and the game descended into a farce.

Although the Celtic incident happened in the year following the World Cup Final, there were players in the Argentina team who were to participate in the Racing Club match against Celtic. So, Alf Ramsey knew what to expect.

Poor behaviour by Argentinians

The England players started the match tentatively. They didn't have long to wait to see what sort of game the Argentinians were going to play. It looked like Rattin was determined to get himself sent off, continuously arguing with referee Kreitlein then, enough was enough, and Rattin had to go, but he wouldn't and soon the whole team was off the field. The fans didn't care they just wanted to win this game. It didn't matter how. For a few minutes it looked like they were not coming back and it was still 0-0. Finally, common sense prevailed. The ten men returned to the field and the battle continued. Then a Geoff Hurst header settled it and the game was over. Onto the next, a much more interesting encounter as Portugal came back from 3-0 down at Goodison Park, to beat the gallant North Koreans 5-3. What a story that would have been! The Koreans had already eliminated Italy.

Stiles v Eusebio

In the Portugal match, it was a matter of keeping Eusebio quiet and Nobby Stiles did just that. Bobby Charlton was the match-winner, scoring two and that was enough, despite Eusebio scoring from a penalty, the first goal England had conceded in 342 minutes of high intensity football. In the Germany v Uruguay match, Captain Troche and Silva of Uruguay, were both sent off to complete a miserable time for the South Americans, as Brazil had been eliminated in the group stage by Portugal. Germany coasted to a 4-0 win to play England for the tenth time, and they hadn't won any of them. They won't have known it, but they are destined to make up for it in the future.

Pelé's injury

In their group match with Portugal, Pelé suffered from one or two malicious tackles, but by that Pelé had already suffered an injury in the previous match against Hungary, and with the score at 2-0, he just had enough, and called time on his 1966 tournament and let the media have its say. This was the only World Cup in which Pelé participated that he didn't win.

Musical greeting

So, the bands were still marching, the crowd still singing, as the teams came out onto the Wembley field, arms swinging, leg-ups and little enthusiastic leaps, trying to remember their manager's last words. After the dignitaries had finished their greetings to the teams and referee Dienst had spun the coin, the game got underway.

Shock lead

On the front foot for the first ten minutes, they suffered a shock after twelve minutes, as with their first attack, the Germans scored. Ray Wilson's header was a gift for Helmut Haller and the Germans were in the lead but only for six minutes as Hurst scored with a header. Then we had to wait for another sixty minutes of great football until Martin Peters scored what we thought was the winning goal but after a free kick against Jack Charlton, the Germans equalised through Wolfgang Weber in the eighty-ninth minute. Into extra-time and then Hursts infamous goal. Was it over the line, did it go in? The debate continues. Most importantly, Swiss referee Gottfried Dienst, after consultation with his Azerbaijani assistant, Tofik Bakhramov, who has a stadium named after him in Azerbaijan, gave a goal.

Then Kenneth Wolstenholme took over:-"........*and here comes Hurst. Some people are on the pitch. They think it's all over. It is now. It's four."*

"I just belted it..." said Hurst. I think he was being modest.

Hurst's goal

The run from the halfway line, after 480 minutes of football in nineteen days, was sensational, leaving a trail of German defenders behind him and running alongside him, screaming for the ball, the only player who could keep up with him, twenty-one year old, Alan Ball, one of the heroes of the tournament.

The party at the Royal Garden Hotel in Kensington, must have gone on for a long time. This was some victory! "Alf was proved right," The newspapers should have added ..."and we got it wrong!"

Conditions of Alf's appointment

When Alf Ramsey was appointed, he insisted on taking control of the selection of the team, which was agreed. He also asked for the disbanding of the International Select Committee, which he considered had no function but he was persuaded to let that one be.

The committee continued, waiting for an opportunity to pounce and they did, seven years later, when England failed to qualify for the 1974 World Cup in Germany. Exit Sir Alf, into obscurity, as he did not have the ability or inclination to use his fame in some other function and bask in the glory of having been the only manager to win the World Cup, up to that time, and probably ever since. Genius is often flawed!

The role of Graham Doggart

He is now a legend, of course, a brilliant footballing brain, a great motivator, as all his players have said, so how did he get appointed by a selection committee consisting of establishment figures who would not be impressed by a man with poor communication skills, with a clipped pseudo upper-class accent. One man stands out and maybe the only one who saw in Alf Ramsey a person who could achieve something which had escaped his predecessor, the much-respected Graham Doggart, Chairman of the Football Association. Walter Winterbottom, sadly, did everything in his power to stop the FA from appointing Alf Ramsey, one of his players from 1950 to 1953.

Winterbottom, ineffectual to the end

In 1962, Winterbottom agreed to step down and run for the Secretary of the Football Association position (which he didn't get) so he was given the job of finding his successor. Alf Ramsey was amongst the applicants but Winterbottom ignored it. He would have known Alf well as a player in the 1950 World Cup and in the Hungary match at Wembley. Never did it occur to him that Alf had the skills to do the job despite his incredible success at Ipswich. After 16 years at the helm, Walter just didn't want to let go and he was looking for someone who would continue to be his subordinate, keeping himself involved in the job he loved. Even in later podcasts at the age of 80, Walter did not realise how hopeless he was in a period when England thought they had the best players in the world. The Hungarians proved them so wrong. So, Alf Ramsey's triumph in 1966 was all the more remarkable, 13 years after that humiliation by the Hungarians. We cover exactly how he did it later but in a word it was pure simplicity and total dedication, exploiting home advantage to the full.

Jimmy Adamson the first choice

Walter had previously recommended Jimmy Adamson who had worked as Assistant Coach with Walter to the 1962 World Cup team, when he was actually part of the squad of players. He continued his coaching duties with England for the next three years whilst still a player with Burnley. Whether this experience was enough to qualify him as coach to the national team, is open to conjecture, as he had no club management experience at all, at this point in his career. Winterbottom was keen to get Adamson on board as this would have ensured his continued involvement with the team, but fortunately the matter was taken out of his hands as Adamason rejected the offer as he did not think he had the required experience and wanted to continue his playing career.

Winterbottom continues to overlook Alf

Seeing that Ramsey was being considered by some of the other members of the FA, Winterbottom became desperate and approached Ron Greenwood, a later England manager, who at that time, had only been coach at West Ham for little over a year so it was clear how misguided Winterbottom was and it was clear also that he didn't want Ramsey.

Watershed Moment

Graham Doggart's key role in appointment

Appointing a successor should never be left to the current incumbent as he will not normally appoint someone who is likely to be more successful than himself so Winterbottom was overruled by some of the elder statesmen at the FA, who understood the mistakes of the past. The search was taken out of Winterbottom's hands by Graham Doggart, Chairman of the Football Association, ex-footballer and cricketer, and Cambridge Blue, who sought the permission of John Cobbold, the Ipswich Chairman, to approach Alf Ramsey in October, 1962, following which the deal was done.

Sadly, Graham Doggart suffered a fatal heart-attack whilst Chairing the Annual Meeting of the Football Association in June,1963, so was unable to witness the fruits of his work. Doggart was clearly the man who had almost single-handedly selected Alf Ramsey and therefore had a key role in the greatest triumph in England's football history.

Winning coach

Sir Alf Ramsey

So how did Alf Ramsay do it? Firstly, he instilled confidence in each of his players by telling them right from the start that they were going to win the World Cup. Also, if you keep telling your players they are the best in the world and are going to win, after a while they start to believe it. Finally, and most importantly he had experienced success in a very unique way. He had taken Ipswich Town from the Third Division in 1957 to the First Division title in 1962, with virtually the same players. No one had ever achieved that before or since.

The only way you can win anything today is by spending millions of pounds on the best players in the world. Ramsey had players like Ray Crawford, who he turned into an England player, Ted Phillips, scorer of 200 plus goals for Ipswich, Jimmy Leadbetter, an average player when he signed him, but he turned him into a key player in the team, and goalkeeper Roy Bailey, the father of Gary Bailey, the ex-Manchester United and England goalkeeper, who had all accompanied Ramsey all the way from the Third Division to the First Division title in five years. The total value in the transfer market for these players was probably no more than twenty-five thousand pounds.

So, Sir Alf had the pedigree. He may also have felt that if he could achieve this feat with Ipswich, a small club with a small budget, doing something similar with the national side when he had the best players at his disposal, better training facilities, access to the best coaches, it should be easier, but then football league clubs, at that time, were not exposed to European and international football, where some of the players had been playing regular international football and were amongst the best players in the world. The national team would have to be prepared to play against players like Pele, Garrincha and Eusebio and that was the biggest challenge facing Ramsey, and his recent trip to Brazil was a reminder of the momentous task ahead.

1966 World Cup Final

30th July 1966

Wembley Stadium, London

England 4 West Germany 2

1962 World Cup

Chile

"Garrincha takes over Pelés role"

"Argentina had done themselves no favours in the eyes of FIFA by refusing to play in 1938, 1950 and 1954, so on reflection, there was no way they were going to allow them to host this one."

Long journey

It amounted to another long journey for the European teams, but it was inevitable that this World Cup would return to South America, Chile being chosen rather than Argentina, who seemed to have all the ingredients but had fallen foul of FIFA.

Earthquake

Two years before the World Cup was due to start, in May,1960, disaster struck when Chile was hit by the most powerful earthquake in history. The country was very familiar with earthquakes and there had been similar occurrences in each of the last three centuries, so FIFA must have been aware of the risks. The earthquake caused considerable damage to buildings and also a huge tsunami which resulted in massive flooding. Several of the stadiums being prepared for the World Cup were damaged and they were left with just four venues.

France, Portugal and Sweden failed to qualify and Austria and Romania decided not to undertake the long journey

Welcome Antonio Rattin

To make matters worse for Argentina, they failed to qualify for the knock-out stage and were defeated by England 3-1 at Rancagua with Greaves and Charlton amongst the scorers. Playing in the Argentina side was the infamous Antonio Rattin, who we were to hear more about in 1966, but only Bobby Charlton and Ray Wilson featured in both the Rancagua and Wembley matches. Uruguay also failed to reach the knock-out stage and like their neighbours Argentina they faced an unpleasant welcome by their fans on returning home.

Pelé's second World Cup

Brazil fielded a twenty-one-year-old Pelé, and eighteen-year-old Coutinho and a thirty-three-year-old Didi, who, unfortunately didn't make it to England in 1966. Italy also failed to advance and included in their squad was an eighteen-year-old, Gianni Rivera.

Legendary half-back line

Czechoslovakia fielded their legendary half back line of Masopust, Pluskal and Popluhar, who, in the group game with Brazil, urged the referee to stop play to attend to Pele's thigh injury which kept him out of the rest of the tournament. In the Hungary team Grosics, the goalkeeper, was the only survivor of Hungary's famous

1954 team, but they also included a twenty-year-old
Florian Albert.

England, beaten in the quarter-final by two excellent
goals from Garrincha, at Vina del Mar, fielded a twenty-
two-year-old Jimmy Greaves, a twenty-one-year-old
Bobby Moore and a twenty-four-year-old Bobby
Charlton.

Battle of Santiago

The match of the tournament, for all the wrong reasons,
was the Chile v Italy encounter, the Battle of Santiago.
Three red cards, punches thrown by both sides
throughout the game all because it seems an Italian
newspaper had called Santiago a "dump, where the
phones don't work and taxis are as rare as faithful
husbands." Apparently, this was not the only derogatory
statement made in the press by Italian journalists, and
there was clearly a history of resentment between the
two countries.

Another win for Brazil with Garrincha the star man

Brazil and Czechoslovakia made it to the final after
tough encounters against Chile and Yugoslavia in the
semi-finals but the Czechs were no match for the star-
studded Brazil team even without Pelé, whose
replacement, Amarildo, scored one of the goals in the 3-
1 win so, Brazil had won successive titles. Garrincha
was the star player of the tournament and he dazzled
time and time again on the right wing. His two goals

knocked out a strong England team and he was a continual threat in every game.

Watershed moment

The last of two legends, Di Stefano and Puskas

Spain, in their group games against Brazil, Mexico and Czechoslovakia included the legendary figure of Ferenc Puskas, the captain of the amazing Hungarian team, who went 42 matches undefeated from 1952 to 1954. Puskas was transferred to Real Madrid following the Hungarian revolution of 1956 and was awarded Spanish citizenship shortly afterwards. Puskas finished with 625 career goals in 629 matches. Also in their squad was Alfredo Di Stefano who had a minor injury and was not called upon in these matches. Di Stefano left his home country, Argentina, in 1949 to play for the Colombian team, Millionarios, well known in England for signing Neil Franklin and Charlie Mitten in 1953. He signed for Real Madrid in 1954 and scored over 200 goals for the club and also became a Spanish citizen. In the 1960 European Cup Final at Hampden Park, in front of a crowd of 127,000, both Di Stefano and Puskas featured for Real Madrid in the 7-3 win over Eintracht Frankfurt, Di Stefano scoring three goals and Puskas four. Their appearances in the Spanish squad in 1962 marked the end of both international careers.

Winning coach

Aymoré Moreira

*Moreira played for the Brazilian national team as a
goalkeeper in the 1930s and managed no less than 30
Brazilian club sides during his lengthy career. He was
appointed to the Brazilian managerial role on the
departure of Vicente Feola and is known for his
attacking play and astute management of his playes.
Vicente Feola regained the coaching role for the 1966
World Cup but Brazil turned again to Moreira following
their poor performance in England.*

1962 World Cup Final

17th June 1962

Estadio Nacional, Santiago

Brazil 3 Czechoslovakia 1

1958 World Cup

Sweden

"The emergence of a 17-year-old kid called Pelé"

Protests from South America

Despite protests from Mexico, Chile and Argentina, who all bid to host the event, Sweden was selected to host the 1958 World Cup. To appease the South Americans, FIFA chose Chile as the 1962 hosts, although with each World Cup now there were an increasing number of countries who were seeing the staging of the event as a way of developing their economy, creating opportunities in business, tourism, real estate and giving the country centre stage not just for the duration of the tournament but also throughout the qualification period.

FIFA achievement

FIFA can take credit for the successful globalisation of the event and with television soon to be available world-wide in most households, the increase in sponsorship opportunities will also provide them with the finance to improve the event's infrastructure and global credibility.

Jules Rimet, the father of the World Cup

Jules Rimet managed to restore the credibility of FIFA in the eyes of the Football Association, and, he was, of course, responsible for launching the World Cup, which will always carry his name and most importantly, he succeeded in transforming it into the successful organisation it is today.

Jules Rimet retired in 1954, after thirty years of immense achievement, but the next two Presidents, Rodolphe Seeldrayers and Arthur Drewry both died in office, but not before the latter had ensured that England finally had its opportunity of hosting the 1966 World Cup. Drewry was succeeded by Sir Stanley Rous, who was to remain President for twelve years so, ironically, the British were back in control of the very organisation they had tried to ditch in 1904.

Mighty Magyars

Leading up to the 1958 World Cup we had observed the unstoppable football passion emerging from South America but could one of their teams achieve victory for the first time outside their own continent? We had also observed the emergence of Hungary, the most talented of all European teams, but only for a period of four years, as tragically their amazing team had been seriously impacted by their country's political events in 1956.

1954 the one the Hungarians should have won

Their supremacy will be hotly disputed by the West Germans, of course, as they had defeated them in the 1954 final, but, unfortunately for the Germans, this World Cup will always be known as the one the Hungarians should have won rather than for the team that won it. Statistics, not publicly recorded, in that era, show that the Hungarians had twenty-six shots on goal with sixteen on target in the final, a good measure of their superiority, but as we see in every game we watch today, possession is not the key. It's goals that count and if you concede three goals as Hungary did, then it's an uphill battle to win the match.

All four Home Nations qualify for the first and maybe last time

The initial shock was the failure to qualify by two-time champions Italy but the biggest pre-tournament success was the qualification of all four Home Nation teams, England, Scotland, Wales and Northern Ireland, the first time this had happened before or since. Two-time winners, Uruguay, also failed to qualify along with Spain and Belgium but it was a welcome back to Argentina, who agreed to participate for the first time since 1934.

Argentina's splendid isolation

As mentioned in another chapter, like England, Argentina also suffered a splendid isolation. Their absence from the World Cup from 1934 to 1958, firstly did them no favours with FIFA and secondly, the absence of competitive international football caused a decline in their performances, exactly as had happened to England. Where England claimed that their Home Nations tournament was the equal of the World Cup in the 1930s, Argentina likewise claimed that their Campeonato Sudamericano was sufficient for them and they also did not wish to play in the same tournament as neighbouring countries with whom they had political disagreements.

In the 1958 tournament Argentina failed to qualify for the knock-out stage and suffered their worst defeat in their World Cup history at the hands of Czechoslovakia 6-1 in a group game played at Helsingborg, which placed them at the bottom of their group.

McParland's five goals

Scotland were one of the first teams to be eliminated following defeats by France and Paraguay but Wales and Northern Ireland qualified for the knock-out stage, Wales, by drawing all three games against Sweden, Hungary and Mexico, and then defeating Hungary, not quite the team of 1954, in a play-off. Peter McParland, the Northern Irish winger scored all five of his country's goals, which must have established some sort of record.

Big decision for Winterbottom

England also drew all three games against Brazil, Soviet Union and Austria, but were defeated in a play-off against the Soviet Union. For the play-off match, the England coach, Walter Winterbottom, had a choice for the centre forward position between Derek Kevan, Bobby Smith and Bobby Charlton, just twenty at the time. He chose Kevan but with the benefit of hindsight, he may have made a mistake. Charlton was already a star at home and apparently when Walter was greeted by his

family at the airport on the way home, his five year-old
son asked "Dad, why didn't you pick Bobby Charlton?"
Even a five year-old knew more about football than
Walter!

Pelé had scored one of his classic goals to eliminate
Wales, but it was not until the semi-final that his real
talent emerged, scoring two goals in their defeat of
France 5-2, whose striker Just Fontaine created a record
of thirteen goals which has stood ever since, and a
further two goals in the final against Sweden, also by a
5-2 margin.

Garrincha

In the final, they fell behind to an early goal by the
Swedish team, managed by George Raynor, but we then
witnessed the arrival of another football genius – the
amazing Garrincha, who, twice in five minutes, waltzed
past his full back to create two goals for Vavá. The
remainder of the game was just a show of sheer brilliant
football.

The Brazilians had reached their summit and were there
to stay as every future World Cup would feature the
same display of talent, Year after year they were the
favourites and the number one ranked team in the world
but of course, as we saw in 1954, the most talented team
doesn't always win in football.

George Raynor

The Football Association will have observed the performance of the Swedish team, their team spirit and the skills shown by their leading players, four of whom were with Serie A clubs in Italy and will certainly have taken note that the coach responsible for getting them to the World Cup final, after winning the Olympic title in 1948 was none other than an Englishman, George Raynor, who, like Jimmy Hogan had been considered by the Football Association as some sort of traitor for coaching a foreign team.

Manager under threat

Having witnessed another failure by the England team, this World Cup could possibly have marked the time when the FA were seriously considering making a management change and many considered that Winterbottom's time was up. Their failure to win key matches had shown unmistakably that other teams were better prepared both physically and mentally and possessed a more ruthless approach to their game, which of course, up to now, was alien to England's way of approaching international tournaments.

One more time for Winterbottom

The FA had finally woken up and had now agreed with the media that a coach with club management experience would be more likely to succeed in restoring the public's faith in the national team but at the next FA meeting, the intransigence and complacency set in again and they decided to stay with Winterbottom, who was more of an establishment figure but someone they trusted implicitly. However, with the next World Cup to be staged in South America again, with Brazil virtually unbeatable, what real chance did they have of winning the trophy?

Watershed moment

The emergence of the wonder kid

The 1954 World Cup will be known for the incredible skills paraded by Puskas, Kocsis, Bozsik and Czibor but whatever impact they made, it was nothing compared to the impact a seventeen-year-old from Brazil made in Sweden in 1958. What the general public wouldn't have known when they first caught sight of Pelé, who looked like young child, was that he had already scored over fifty league and cup goals for Santos, the first one at the age of fifteen. His Brazilian coaches could not have been confident that he would escape the ruthless tackling that Brazil had experienced in 1954, but they need not have worried. He moved so fast no one could catch him. In the 1960s, Pelé, apart from his triumphs with the national team, was to turn the small coffee port of Santos, into the no 1 football club in the world, winning two Inter-Continental Cups, which was played between the champions of South America and the champions of Europe. By the age of twenty-one Pelé had scored over 300 goals for club and country and finished with 640 goals in 660 matches. Unfortunately, he never played in

Europe except for the 1958 World Cup but his dazzling skills in Sweden were there for all to see. By the time of the 1970 World Cup, Pelé was past his best, despite leading Brazil to a third World Cup and when he signed for the New York Cosmos, in 1975, it would probably be the first time he was able to make any real money.

Winning coach

Vicente Feola

Apart from winning Brazil's first World Cup, Feola can be credited with giving seventeen-year-old Pelé his debut in the 1958 World Cup, when he rewarded his mentor by scoring six goals in his first four matches. Feola successfully managed Sao Paulo FC for a total of twenty-one years from 1937 at the age of twenty-eight until he was appointed coach to the Brazilian team in 1958. He returned as coach to the Brazilian team for the1966 World Cup in England when he was heavily criticised for changing virtually his whole defence including goalkeeper for the match against Portugal at Goodison Park which eliminated Brazil from the tournament, as well as playing a half-fit Pelé who had to leave the field early in the second half.

1958 World Cup Final

29th June 1958

Rasunda Stadium, Solna

Brazil 5 Sweden 2

1954 World Cup

Switzerland

"The end of the road for the Magical Magyars"

"The final featured the biggest turnaround in World Cup history, before or since as West Germany had conceded eight goals to Hungary in their group game."

Historic event for Switzerland

The hosts had been selected, principally due to their neutrality in the war and commitment to construct brand-new stadiums for the finals. Switzerland was a smaller country with chosen World Cup venues closer together so would not involve lengthy inter-city travelling experienced by some of the teams in Brazil.

Hungarians the favourites

Preceding events were sure to make this one of the more entertaining tournaments. The Hungarians had demolished England in 1953 and a few weeks before the World Cup was due to start, in the return fixture in Budapest, handed out England's biggest ever defeat, 7-1. As a result of these victories and their triumph in the recent Olympic Games, they were overwhelming favourites to win the tournament. Hungary were also in the middle of a twenty-four match unbeaten run.

Argentina stay at home again

The Swedish, Spanish and Japanese teams had all failed to qualify and the Argentinians had again preferred to stay at home - still refusing to participate in an event in which their Brazilian neighbours were also playing.

Hungary started impressively with an 8-3 victory over West Germany, who had rested some of their key players in anticipation of a play-off game with Turkey, which they managed to win, so both teams progressed to the quarter finals. Also progressing were England and Uruguay who had met in Montevideo the previous year.

Uruguay defeat Scotland and England

Uruguay had been far too good for Scotland in their group game and ran out winners by 7-0, with the Scot's lack of experience at this level being ruthlessly exposed by the South Americans. England, fresh from the Hungarian debacle, played a more inspiring tournament before losing the quarter-final 4-2 which left Uruguay still in the running for a third successive World Cup triumph.

Uruguay number one ranked team

Ironically, back in 1920, the two highest ranked teams in the world would have been Scotland and England, probably in that order. Uruguay, by virtue of winning the 1924 and 1928 Olympic Games titles, followed by the World Cup in 1930, would have taken over the top spot and here we are in 1954, and Uruguay consolidating their position by demolishing both countries, and in both matches they were unmistakably superior. South American football had arrived.

The Battle of Bern

As had often happened in the World Cup, the best teams can be drawn together in an earlier round and so it was with the trophy holders, Brazil, the leading South American team, and the indisputable leading European team, Hungary. What a prospect! It did not disappoint but became known as "The Battle of Bern," and rather than a match of beauty as everyone had hoped, it developed into a physical battle. Hungary emerged as the winners, 4-2, after three players had been sent off. They then managed to eliminate Uruguay, in the semi-final, without the injured Puskas.

Austria return to the World Cup

West Germany defeated the rejuvenated Austria team 6-1, in their semi-final, the same Austrian team who had achieved a remarkable 7-5 win against the hosts in the previous round, still the largest aggregate score in the history of the World Cup but, over the two rounds, they had succeeded in conceding eleven goals, a bit of a headache for their coaching team. However, Austria must have been thankful that following their annexation in 1938, they were now back in the World Cup in their own name.

Westdeutschland gewinnt zum ersten Mal

The final featured the biggest turnaround in World Cup history, before or since. West Germany, who had conceded eight goals to Hungary in their group game, were 2-0 down in the final, after ten minutes, but amazingly managed to turn things around on a rain-sodden pitch and emerged 3-2 winners. The Hungarian claim that the German squad were taking amphetamines is now gaining more acceptance as substantial evidence has recently emerged of drug-taking in sport in Germany during that era. However, FIFA had no rules regarding doping at that time so the West Germans could not have been punished.

Avoiding Hungary again

England would have had no confidence coming into the tournament and elimination by Uruguay in the quarter-finals was not surprising but the result conveniently avoided another England v Hungary match in the semi-finals, as this would probably have brought further heartache as Hungary had now, on two separate occasions, demonstrated their superiority in virtually every department of their game.

"Jimmy Hogan taught us everything"

Regarding the performances of Hungary, the Football Association must have been wondering how the country England defeated 6-2 in 1936 had reached this level of technical ability. Much of the credit has been given to

Jimmy Hogan, who started his playing career at Burnley and then set off on a coaching career in a number of European countries including Hungary and Austria, who both became leading footballing nations in the 1930s.

After Hungary's famous victory at Wembley, their President, Sandor Barcs, had remarked: - "Jimmy Hogan taught us everything we know about football." Hogan spent the latter part of his career in the football league but was not as successful as he had been in other parts of Europe. How much this was due to genuine failure or finding his coaching techniques too practical is open to question.

England's fate

As far as England are concerned each tournament seems to reveal how much more they have fallen behind. Maybe there is an excuse for the tournament held in Brazil, the first time the team had travelled to South America and also the vital game against Spain played in front of a hostile crowd. However, it had been followed by two disastrous performances against Hungary, and now a missed opportunity to redeem themselves against a Uruguayan team who were playing in unfamiliar territory in Europe.

Watershed moment

Hungarian revolution

Hungary's supremacy in football was soon to end. Their progress was halted by the 1956 revolution, which resulted in Soviet occupation of the country. Puskas, Kocsis and Czibor all left for Spain and that incredible 1954 team was no more, although Hungary's amateurs did manage to win two Olympic titles in the 1960s. The defeat by West Germany would have been a great shock to them, as they were just not used to losing. Their 42-match unbeaten run ended at the Wankdorf Stadium.

Winning coach

Sepp Herberger

Another unsung hero, he coached the German team to one of the biggest upsets in the history of the World Cup, when his team defeated the legendary Hungarian team, in the "miracle of Bern." The result was even more amazing as Hungary had defeated the Germans 8-3 in the group stage, when they were firing on all cylinders, but in the final, like Brazil and Argentina before them, they just ran out of steam. Herberger also reached the semi-finals in the 1958 World Cup in Sweden and the quarter-finals in Chile in 1962.

1954 World Cup Final

4th July 1954

Wankdorf Stadium, Bern

West Germany 3 Hungary 2

1950 World Cup

Brazil

"200,000 fans had turned up to witness the biggest sporting celebration in the country's history. Instead, they experienced an absolute disaster."

Argentina disagreement with Brazil

Thankfully, the war was over for the European countries, although some of the protagonists, Germany and Japan were banned for the World Cup in Brazil and USSR and other Eastern European countries chose not to enter. France, Scotland, Argentina and India for different reasons also pulled out, France because of the amount of travelling required between the group games and Argentina allegedly because Brazil failed to honour an agreement for their neighbours to host one or two of the games. Scotland had announced that they would only go to Brazil if they had won the Home Internationals but failed to do so and India pulled out for financial reasons or, as some would have it, because they weren't permitted to play barefooted.

Korean war takes the headlines

England, on their first South American visit, with Alf Ramsey, future coach of the national team, in their squad, started well by defeating Chile at the Maracanã Stadium, then a bout of the usual complacency set in as four days later they suffered a result which shook the footballing world, just as Harry Truman, the US President had announced he was preparing to send US troops into Korea. Against all the odds, the USA team consisting of part-time footballers, on a bumpy pitch, in front of a meagre crowd, in Belo Horizonte, with few journalists there to record the event, succeeded in defeating the England national team 1-0 with the goal, a deflected header, scored by Joe Gaetjens, who was later kidnapped and never seen again.

The end of an era of dominance

It was too much to take for the media. Years of arrogance, complacency, "splendid isolation," the pretence that they were still the dominant force in world football, were all going up in smoke. Like Brazil in 1938, they had rested their key player for the match, in this case, Stanley Matthews, one of the world's most talented footballers. Many, many excuses were given - they were pressured to participate against their will, the players were not properly prepared for the flight, the pitch they played on was not of the required standard for an international match, the referee was maybe not biased but incompetent. The excuses just went on and on but the fact remained, England and the FA had been humiliated. It was only the start of a long line of disasters that were about to hit the national team, but this was the one that hurt and if they had managed to win their next game, the USA result would probably have been forgotten. However, it was not to be as Spain eliminated England a few days later and so the England squad together with their coach and the FA representatives attending, prepared for the long journey back home to face the media.

More humiliation

Having qualified for the final group, Spain were beaten 6-1 by Brazil so, if England had qualified for the knock-out stage instead of Spain, they could have experienced even more humiliation as it was clear that the team they brought to Brazil was totally unprepared for a tournament of this magnitude.

Another major shock

Meanwhile, in the other groups, Sweden, managed by English coach George Raynor, also qualified for the knock-out stage, but after a good run, were eliminated by the eventual winners, Uruguay and if England's loss to the USA was, up to then, the major shock of the tournament, this was nothing compared to the shock suffered by 200,000 fans at the Maracanã Stadium when Uruguay overcame Brazil in the final.

Poor Moacyr

They used to say that never a day went by when fans didn't recall that fateful day and poor Moacyr Barbosa, the Brazilian goalkeeper was haunted for the rest of his life by the winning goal he conceded at his near post, eleven minutes from time. The only consolation for Barbosa, who has long since passed on, is that he didn't experience the world of social media that we all have to live with today, as he would have been subjected to serial abuse.

That never-to-be-forgotten day

Brazilians never, ever forgot the 1950 World Cup, despite having won several World Cups since. It is firmly etched into their memories as the most disastrous day in their football history. What was so different about the 1950 final was that 200,000 fans had turned up to witness the biggest sporting celebration in the country's history. Instead, they experienced an absolute disaster. It was an example of *paixao brasileira* gone hopelessly wrong.

Of the five World Cups that Brazil have won none of them have been in front of their delirious fans on home soil.

No lessons learned

As for England, their memories of the USA match would slowly dim as they were to suffer much more significant defeats in the next few years. Most importantly, however, it would appear that, despite the incredible experience of playing at the Maracanã and watching the best teams in the world, at the same time being in a position to observe the results of more technical coaching methods, the players and the team of coaches and officials who attended the finals, learned absolutely nothing from this latest episode in England's football history.

Splendid isolation yet again?

Was it pure arrogance or was it a feeling of inferiority starting to develop, as it was very clear that the South Americans and some of the leading European teams were well ahead of England in terms of technical ability? It was to become even more evident over the next four years that the period of "splendid isolation" had done irreparable damage to the British psyche and caused utter confusion in the minds of the FA, who now had a choice between treating this Brazilian experience as a one-off with all the many excuses or, grasping the nettle, tackling the issue face-on, and admitting that they were no longer one of the leading nations in the country's national pastime.

George Reader, one of the *English* referees selected for the *World Cup* quotes *"My powers of control were put to the test straight away after Brazil scored their first goal against Mexico, which heralded a mass invasion of reporters demanding immediate responses from both the goal scorer and goalkeeper, as was customary at the time."*

Watershed moment

Torino tragedy

The draw did include Italy, the last winners of the Jules Rimet trophy in 1938, despite their leading league team,

Torino, having been a victim, in 1949, of one of the most tragic events in football history, when their whole squad of thirty-one players, coaches, officials, and journalists perished when their Italian Airlines flight crashed into the Basilica of Superga in Turin. Torino were the leading Italian club and had won four Serie A league titles in the 1940s. Seven of the Torino team would have been in the Italian squad so the national team were clearly weakened in this World Cup, had no chance of winning a third World Cup title and were eliminated at the group stage.

Winning coach

Juan Lopez succeeded where many failed by defeating Brazil at the Maracanã stadium where they had never previously been defeated in a competitive match. In fact, such is the magnitude of the task confronting opponents at the Maracanã, Brazil went thirty years before another team beat them at this historic stadium. Juan Lopez's mentor had been Alberto Suppici, 1930 winning coach, who clearly had a role in appointing Lopez in 1946. The features of the South American teams of this era were speed, agility and ruthless tackling, much like today. However, as in 1930, the Uruguayans' success was due to their second half performance. In both matches, 1930 and 1950, Uruguay came from behind, after conceding the first goal, to win the World Cup. Lopez also took Uruguay to the semi-finals of the 1954 World Cup in Switzerland and also played a role in the 1962 World Cup in Chile and the 1970 World Cup in 1970, where

Uruguay again reached the semi-final, so with one win and two semi-final appearances, Lopez, although somewhat of an unsung-hero, can be considered one the most successful managers in World Cup history. However, the golden era for Uruguayan football was approaching the end and although they reached the semi-final in 1954, that would be the last time for the next 68 years.

1950 World Cup Final

16th July, 1950

Maracaña Stadium, Rio de Janeiro

Uruguay 2 Brazil 1

1938 World Cup

France

"Although Europe was heading for another disastrous conflict, the World Cup event, now in its third year, was beginning to receive universal acclaim."

Annexation of Austria

Mussolini had eliminated his opposition parties some years ago, Franco had, by now, been responsible for the death of thousands of Spanish people caught up in the Civil War and Hitler had not only conducted a purge on members of his own Nazi party, (*The Night of the Long Knives*), he had also annexed Austria (the *Anschluss*) and merged Austria's football team into his own, which would mean Germany had acquired one the best players in Europe, Matthias Sindelar. Or so they thought, as Sindelar refused to play for Germany and died in mysterious circumstances in 1939. This also meant that Austria, one of the most successful teams in Europe, the *Wunderteam* of the 1930s, coached by Hugo Meisl, would no longer be able to participate in the tournament in their own name.

Political platform

Italy had won the previous tournament in their home country and also the Olympic Games title in Germany in 1936. Mussolini's plan to use the tournaments as a platform to promote his political party seemed to be working but he seemed to be getting desperate and had allegedly left a message for the Italian players before the final in Paris "win or die!" Thankfully, future World Cup teams were not about to adopt Mussolini's cynical approach.

There were no refereeing scandals but FIFA will have learned that sending teams home after one loss in a knock-out competition was not the best way forward, so each future World Cup would have enough participants to hold a group stage where every nation would have at least three games.

England's mistrust of the fascist states

With mistrust of the fascist states increasing day by day there was no way England were going to enter this tournament, although ironically, this World Cup presented them with their best opportunity as the Matthews/Lawton combination was firing on all cylinders and they had recently recorded a run of resounding victories, defeating Hungary 6-2, Norway 6-0, Sweden 4-0, Finland 8-0, Germany 6-3. This was England's best spell in their history and it was such a tragedy that the FA were so intent on continuing their "splendid isolation," which was beginning to destroy their credibility. The rise of fascism, all around them, did not seem to worry the French, who went about the organisation of the tournament in exemplary fashion.

Mysterious decision by the FA

The Football Association had rejected FIFA's invitation to participate in this particular World Cup based on their concern about the rise of fascism in some of the competing countries, but here they were in a fixture against their bête noire, Germany, three weeks before the start of the World Cup, giving them a Nazi salute just one year before Germany invaded Poland and started World War II.

Reminder of things to come from Brazilians

The other highlight of the World Cup was the performance of the Brazilian team, whose football enthralled passionate French fans and was a clear indication of things to come in the 1950s when Brazil began their domination of world football. Their star player in 1938 was Leonidas, scorer of seven goals in the finals, whose manager Adhemar Pimenta decided to rest for the semi-final against Italy, in preparation for the final. It proved to be an unwise decision, Brazil lost their semi-final and Pimenta was axed.

Italy then won an entertaining game against Hungary (perhaps a warning of things to come) in the final by four goals to two. Italy were to retain the trophy for a further twelve years until the 1950 World Cup in Brazil, as in a short time, the world would be at war again and football's further development would be put on hold.

Watershed moment

Nazi salute

In May, 1938, just three weeks before the commencement of the World Cup in France, England played Germany in Berlin, emerging with a 6-3 victory. Adding to the hypocrisy of this fixture, as the teams lined up before the match, each of the England players gave the Nazi salute, the British government later announcing that the gesture was a plan to appease Hitler as they were still hoping for peace. Whether this is true or not, the picture of the England team giving the salute has gone viral and turned the game in Berlin into one more humiliating event for the Football Association.

Winning coach - for the second time

Vittorio Pozzo

This was another triumph for the Italian team, in particular for their coach, Vittorio Pozzo, who had succeeded in coaching Italy to two successive World Cup victories, a record that still stands today. Pozzo coached the Italian national team for a total of nineteen years and attained legendary status both at home and abroad.

1938 World Cup Final

19th June 1938

Stade Olympique de Colombe, Paris

Italy 4 Hungary 2

1934 World Cup

Italy

"Mussolini takes control of his Italian stallions"

Italy transformed

With Europe careering towards another world war, European leaders were already beginning to choose their alliances. Mussolini had already transformed Italy into a fascist dictatorship and had eliminated all opposition parties. It quickly became apparent when Italy was awarded the World Cup that he was going to use it as a political platform to promote his fascist regime - also that he was going to take complete control of the football team and most of the administrative decisions.

Bidding for host country

After failing to secure a European host for the 1930 World Cup, FIFA's clear objective was to pave the way for a country nearer home to take control of the next one. Sweden was the only other bidder but they were soon swept away by the strength and power of the Italian bid.

Innovations

Italy had decided to play the games in different cities around the country, probably for political purposes, but this idea was to stay with the World Cup and later the European Championships for the next eight decades.

Strangely, the 1930 policy of playing all the games in one city went full circle after a period of 92 years as the 2022 World Cup in Qatar was also staged in one city and played at a number of stadiums in the city of Doha. In 1934, as more than thirty nations had applied to participate in the World Cup, there needed to be a qualification process for the sixteen agreed places. This policy was also adopted by all future World Cup hosts.

Home not alone

The first shock exits were Brazil and Argentina and as the competition consisted of a knock-out from the first round without any group games, their players were on the way home after just one game apiece. France, Netherlands and Belgium followed them home shortly afterwards also after just one game. Luis Monti, the star Argentinian captain in Montevideo, was now in the Italian squad together with two other players poached from Argentina's successful 1930 team.

Advent of fascism

Many European countries had been wary of political moves Mussolini was making and the progress Spain and Germany were achieving in transforming their nations into fascist states. Hitler was about to take over as German Chancellor, Franco was about to take Spain into a civil war and Mussolini was already a fascist dictator who was not to be trusted, so this was not the World Cup for any of the British teams, FIFA members or not."

The continued success of Vittorio Pozzo

Italy, taken to extra-time in the semi-final, defeated Spain, who had been the very first foreign team to beat England in Madrid in May,1929. This was followed by several more defeats for England in the 1930s as the European teams all turned professional and hired qualified club coaches, leaving England, as surely the only leading footballing nation in the 1930s, without an established coach. Italy, since 1929, had employed the highly celebrated Vittorio Pozzo, who served as Italy's coach for a total of nineteen years, and was instrumental in winning the 1934 World Cup, the1936 Olympic football tournament in Germany and the 1938 World Cup in France. England weren't learning anything, just sitting on the side-lines, watching the world of football pass them by.

For the record, in the 1934 final, Italy defeated Czechoslovakia, again after extra-time, so Mussolini was able to celebrate a famous victory.

Watershed moment

Each World Cup has its scandals and this one produced the first one of any significance. Italy, after very close games with Spain and Austria, had won an enthralling encounter with Czechoslovakia in the final and would have won universal acclaim but for the fact that the Swedish referee, Erik Eklind, was chosen to officiate both Italy's semi-final and final matches, a unique occurrence in the World Cup. This left Italy wide open to suggestions of corruption as it was alleged (without any substantiation), that Mussolini held a meeting with Eklind before the final.

Winning coach

Vittorio Pozzo

Putting Mussolini's involvement to one side, the central figure of this World Cup and for the next twenty years was Italy's coach, Vittorio Pozzo, who managed the national team in the 1924 Olympics, the 1934 and 1938 World Cups and continued right up to 1948. Pozzo coached during a torrid time for Italian football. Never being able to refuse any orders given by Mussolini, he was accused later of being a fascist, the Nazi salute given by the Italian team, dressed in all-black gear, in 1938, attracting derision from anti-fascists, and although he never admitted publicly to any political beliefs, his place in Italian football history is still open to question. He remains the only manager to have won two World Cups in succession.

1934 World Cup Final

10ᵗʰ June 1934

Stadio Nazionale, Rome

Italy 2 Czechoslovakia 1

1930 World Cup

Uruguay

"Uruguay's bid was accepted at a FIFA meeting in Barcelona in 1929, with probably a little trepidation. Refusing their bid might have resulted in the abandonment of the World Cup."

Expenses claim

With football having become professional in Britain and the rest of Europe soon to follow, and also after suspicions that some European countries were paying their players generous expenses at the Olympic Games of 1924 and 1928, FIFA, now the recognised governing body for football, took the next step in the globalisation of football by deciding to launch the World Cup.

Original plans

The intention of Jules Rimet, the President of FIFA, had clearly been to appoint one of the European countries to host the first event in 1930 and then bank on its North and South American members agreeing to undertake the long sea voyage to Europe as he would, of course, have known that USA, Mexico, Argentina, Uruguay and Brazil had made a successful trip to Paris and Amsterdam in 1924 and 1928 for the Olympic Games. However, the reverse happened as the four initial European bidders, withdrew one by one, when they began to understand the costs involved. Also. none of their bids had been able to match the bid of Uruguay, who offered a more realistic package, were prepared to construct a stadium especially for the event and later agreed to finance some of the countries who had been suffering financial difficulties due to the 1929 Stock Market collapse.

Uruguayan independence

Uruguay also intended the event to coincide with the centenary of their independence from the Spanish in 1830. Uruguay had won the Olympic Games football tournament in both 1924 and 1928 and there was an air of confidence in the camp to accompany an air of curiosity at FIFA, as Uruguay was a little-known country with a population of scarcely two million people.

Uruguay's bid confirmed

Uruguay's bid was accepted at a FIFA meeting in Barcelona in 1929, with probably a little trepidation. Refusing their bid might have resulted in the abandonment of the World Cup, as if FIFA had insisted on a European host, this may have brought about a withdrawal of all the South American teams. So, FIFA had no alternative but to accept Uruguay's plans.

However, problems soon began to arise. After initial interest, the countries whose bids had been rejected, pulled out one by one. Playing in an event hosted in Europe was one thing but embarking on a two-week sea voyage to South America was another and it was quite amazing that the event got off the ground at all. Most of the other South American countries had no hesitation and signed up immediately, USA and Mexico also. Egypt literally missed the boat, having arrived too late for their connecting steamship in Marseille and had no other way of reaching Montevideo in time for the tournament.

British clubs' tours

There were very good reasons that many of FIFA's member countries decided to miss the first World Cup. In England's case, Southampton had toured South America in 1904, Tottenham Hotspurs in 1909, Exeter City in 1914 and Chelsea in 1929. None of the teams ventured a second tour due to crowd violence and the brutal antics of some their opponents, so the FA already had an idea of what to expect in Uruguay. Many of the other nations were still playing amateur football and a two week voyage each way by steamship meant at least two months off work for their players which was just not feasible.

Sea voyage

As deadlines approached, it looked like the stadium would not be ready for the first game on 13th July as heavy rain had delayed construction. But the major difficulty was getting European teams on board and many of the leading teams Italy, Spain, Netherlands, Belgium were still amateur which meant players having to take considerable time off work, with the cost of the sea voyage, hotel and subsistence for each of the players having to be financed also. FIFA would have been aware of these issues at the Barcelona meeting which supports the argument that there was no other option available other than Uruguay.

World Cup 1930 gets under way

Eventually France, Belgium, Romania and Yugoslavia agreed to participate after Uruguay had agreed to meet some of the costs. So, following the historic, initial match between France and Mexico, the first World Cup got under way and thankfully, the stadium was ready for Uruguay's first match against Peru, exactly 100 years from their independence from Spain on 18th July, 1830.

Uruguay v Argentina final

The players would have no idea at the time of the significance of the tournament, marking the commencement of a journey towards what would be known as the greatest event in sporting history. Thirteen competing nations finally lined up for the tournament with Uruguay and Argentina, based on their performances in the Olympic Games, being the undisputed favourites as the four European teams would not have been able to bring all of their best players and so it was no surprise when the two leading South American teams met in the final. Brazil could have reached the final but that was clearly not the plan so the Uruguayan officials provided a Uruguayan referee for

Brazil's group game against Yugoslavia which put an
end to their hopes of upsetting the Uruguay Argentina
party. Uruguay defeated Argentina 4-2 in the final,
which according to reports was an exhilarating game,
both teams displaying the usual South American flair
and passion.

Successful USA team

One of the successes of the tournament was the USA
team, assembled at the last moment and consisting
mostly of part-time professionals who had never
previously played together. They succeeded in beating
Belgium 3-0 and Paraguay by the same score, reaching
the semi-final for the first and only time in their history
and finally being eliminated by a vastly superior
Argentinian team. They played three matches in Brazil
on the way home, were popular throughout the tour, and
the trip to South America was a highly successful public
relations exercise for the American Football Association.

Aftermath

The matches had gone ahead without great incident.
There were some dubious refereeing decisions
accompanied by the usual South American crowd
violence and some vicious tackling, in particular by Luis
Monti, Argentina's brutal centre-half, later to be poached
by Juventus and selected to play for Italy in the 1934
World Cup. Uruguay, however, can be proud of their
place in football history although they chose not to
participate in the next two World Cups held in Italy and

France, supposedly in reaction to the poor response from European nations to their World Cup. It could also have been partly for the same financial reasons which caused the European countries to opt out. Ironically, at the very next World Cup in which Uruguay participated in 1950, they won again, and then reached the semi-finals in 1954.

A further example of "splendid isolation?"

So, the Football Association had no interest in participating in the 1930 World Cup, despite a last-minute invitation, but what would have happened if they had travelled to Uruguay? Would they have bonded well with the Belgian, French and Romanian teams on board the steamship that transported them to Montevideo? Probably, as all the passengers would have found the whole experience of their first sea voyage incredibly exciting.

1930 World Cup a successful experiment

This World Cup served as little more than an experiment, albeit a successful one. It was FIFA's first attempt to globalise football and bring teams together in an official tournament, and they would have learned from the experience. By 1934, most of FIFA's members had become professional so the cost of participating would be less of a burden than it was in 1930, but until trans-continental air travel was available, universal endorsement of the World Cup could not be possible.

Refereeing and crowd behaviour

They wouldn't have been comfortable with the standard of refereeing at the games, however, and also the passionate South American fans who were at times uncontrollable. That could have drawn the players into unsavoury incidents and the attitude of the FA of that era would have been to call time on any game that was getting out of control, so realistically, the FA was not in the right frame of mind to undergo such an examination of their behaviour at such events. so,

Despite the relative success of the first World Cup in difficult circumstances, FIFA was probably pleased to get the whole thing over with and looked forward to the next World Cup, hosted by Mussolini's Italy.

One of the reasons the British sporting press gave the event so little coverage was because the World Cup finals coincided with a highly entertaining Ashes Test series. The excitement of the Uruguayan fans following their nation's victory would probably have been matched by the Australian cricket fans as the lucky ones watched and others read about their twenty-one-year-old protégé Don Bradman taking the cricketing world by storm in scoring a triple hundred and two double centuries in the series, a feat which has never been repeated.

Watershed moment

Jim Brown

One of USA's most successful players was a twenty-one-year-old Scottish player, Jim Brown, who, shortly after the tournament, travelled back home and was signed by Manchester United, for whom he played forty matches before moving down the divisions and finishing his career at Guildford where he was a prolific goal scorer. Jim's son, George, also played for the USA national team and both have been elected to the USA Soccer Hall of Fame. In the 1994 World Cup, hosted by the USA, Jim Brown was led onto the field for the USA's first match in a wheel chair to greet the teams.

Winning coach

Alberto Suppici

He has the honour of being the first World Cup coach to win the World Cup. Little is known about Suppici's tactical approach to but the energy of the Uruguayan team was a feature of their performance. The last surviving Argentinian player of the 1930 World Cup, Francisco Varallo, who died aged 100 in 2010, when questioned about the final match remarked: "In the second half, we just ran out of steam and they just kept going." Suppici is the first and last coach to drop a player from the squad for disciplinary reasons. First-choice goalkeeper, Andres Mazali broke the curfew established by Suppici before the first match and missed

*the whole World Cup, and never played for Uruguay
again. Suppici won numerous trophies in his two spells
as national team coach, finally retiring in 1941.*

1930 World Cup Final

30th July 1930

Estadio Centenario, Montevideo

Uruguay 4 Argentina 2

Appendix

The Mighty Magyars

"Their style was all about understanding, rhythm and intuition and linked together by the lovely skills and the effect was devastating."- Ron Greenwood

The big match

Their time had come! It was 25th November, 1953. They had won the Helsinki Olympic Games, in 1952, with the same players, but their achievement had not been recognised by the football world, because football at the Olympic Games was no longer a major event since the World Cup emerged in 1930 and also because, of course, the Hungarians were not considered amateurs! That, anyhow, was the opinion of the Football Association. Many of the Hungarians played for Honved, which was the Hungarian army team and they were paid employees of the Hungarian army but any protests would fall on deaf ears so, on this bright, winter's day in London, they had something to prove.

Even though they had been unbeaten in over thirty games, to gain any sort of recognition, they had to beat the so-called masters of the game. The press were mixed in their predictions. There were some who were living in the past, who thought the Hungarians could never handle the hard tackling of the England defence. Walter Winterbottom apparently did not share the enthusiasm.

He had watched the Hungarians in the Olympic Games and he understood the magnitude of the task ahead.

An unforgettable exhibition

England could not have got off to a worse start. Hidegkuti scored in the first minute. Three more came in a fifteen-minute spell in the first half and England never recovered. They managed, somehow, to get enough possession to score three goals but this was an exhibition of football that would long remain in the memory of football fans. It was also the day English football finally lost its supremacy. They could be forgiven for the display in Brazil in 1950, when they had to cope with hostile crowds, poor facilities and badly prepared playing surfaces but this match took place on the sacred Wembley turf, in front of one hundred thousand fans. As for Hungary, they were the newly crowned supremos! Geoffrey Green, writing for The Times:- "England were no longer a major world power in the game."

Hungary in 1930s

Where did it all start? Hungary had only beaten England on one occasion, in 1933, in Budapest, by 2-1, which had some significance, as they were only the third team ever to beat England, following the Spanish and French defeats of 1929 and 1931 so there was a sign, even then, they had some status in European football. In 1931, however, at Highbury, England took revenge on Spain with a 7-1 win.

Hungary's most significant achievement of that era was in the 1938 when they reached the World Cup Final, beating Sweden 5-1 in the semi-final so even as late as 1938, they were a force in world football.

Here we go again

With football crumbling before their very eyes, the last thing England wanted was a repeat of the devastation witnessed in 1953 but in May of the following year, just four weeks before the World Cup, the Football Association had agreed to play Hungary again, this time in Budapest, in front of a crowd of ninety thousand at the Nepstadion.

Whether this was good timing, in view of the humiliation England had suffered a few months before, is open to debate. There could have been people in the football administration who had genuinely felt this was a glitch in England's footballing history and it could never happen again but there will be others who felt this was a big mistake and we will live to regret the result. Well, it turned out to be a grave error of judgment. Hungary cemented their supremacy over England and won 7-1. After sixty-eight minutes, they had just scored four goals in twelve minutes, so they slowed down, not wishing to cause England more pain. The team the selection committee had chosen, contained three players making their debut and were without Ramsey and Johnston, who had played at Wembley, and witnessed the Hungarian tactics at first hand and would surely not have made the same mistakes again. Job done; they had consolidated their supremacy in world football.

The end of an era

However, things were not well at home for Hungary. In 1956, Khrushchev sent in his tanks to crush Hungary's revolution against policies imposed by the Russian government. Puskas and other members of the Honved team were out of the country at the time and never returned. The brief supremacy was over and Hungary would no longer be the eminent force in world football and they would never return. Russian assumption of power in Hungary would have had an effect on not just the players, but also the management, the football administration and ultimately the Hungarian government so there was nothing in place to hold the football team together, and at times like this, sport is the last consideration. The Hungarian people were in fear of their lives and their future and this was the priority.

Three survivors

They managed to assemble a team in June, 1957 but were defeated by Norway in the qualification process for the 1958 World Cup. By November, 1957, however, they defeated Norway 5-0 in Budapest, in the return fixture, to complete their qualification. In Sweden, they failed to get out of their group, drawing with Wales and losing to Sweden. Three members of the 1953/54 team survived the revolution: Grosics, Bozsik and Hidegkuti, who retired immediately after the 1962 World Cup to commence a successful coaching career.

Hungarians still alive

In the 1962 World Cup in Chile, there was just time for one more defeat of England, 2-1 in Rancagua, a 6-0 win against Bulgaria and a draw against Argentina which qualified them for the knock-out stage but they were defeated by the finalists Czechoslovakia.

In 1966, they participated in one of the most entertaining matches in the World Cup, defeating the holders, Brazil 3-1, at Goodison Park, and that was it, except for two gold medals in the Olympic Games in 1964 and 1968 for their amateur team.

Jimmy Hogan hero or villain?

One name who made a major contribution to the development of Hungarian football in its early stages was Jimmy Hogan who was given a significant mention by Gustav Sebes, the Hungarian coach in 1953:- "*We played football as Jimmy Hogan taught us. When our football history is told, his name should be written in gold letters,*" Was this statement pure politics, driving the wedge home, giving the impression that one of England's own coaches had conspired with the Hungarians to create this humiliating moment in English football? Well, it certainly had that effect.

Billy Wright later called Jimmy a traitor. He had tried desperately to gain a footing back in the football league in the mid -1930s but his coaching methods were very basic. He had taken jobs with clubs in Germany, Austria and Hungary in the early 1900s when football was at its very early stages and all that was needed was a coach to teach them kicking, heading and ball control skills but when Jimmy came back to the UK, club football had moved on and his skills were found wanting.

Hungary's success was due, in part, to continual exposure to the leading teams in Eastern Europe in particular the Central European International Cup, which was played over five years in the 1930s and 1950s, when they won it. Their first meeting with England was in the 1912 Olympic Games when they lost 7-0. Well, those two historic wins in 1953 and 1954 certainly avenged that defeat!

Moscow Dynamo 1945

The Football Association had received an earlier warning in 1945 that their football was becoming outmoded. Moscow Dynamo, on a goodwill tour of England, Scotland and Wales, had displayed a brand of football never before witnessed on this island. Apart from finishing the tour unbeaten, they demonstrated a game of quick passing and teamwork that had the huge crowds captivated. *"The Russians were on the move all the time,"* remarked Chelsea full-back Albert Tennant," *We could hardly keep up with them."* This was similar to comments made by England defenders in the Hungary match eight years later.

Journalist, John Chatterton remarks in his report on the Moscow Dynamo tour:-"*The visit of Dynamo Moscow had shown that football in this country was lagging dangerously behind the innovation taking place across the continent.*"

Nothing changed

Hungary were to provide further proof of this, of course, and, again no action was taken by the Football Association. It was clear that the only way to implement a change in the style of play necessary to compete with the world's best teams was a change in the team management, but it took the FA eight years from the Hungarian debacle for them to realize this, despite continual reminders from the press that, however much they respected Walter Winterbottom, he was not the man to implement the required changes. Walter himself must have realized this but not until 1962, in Chile, after witnessing Brazil's demolition of England, did he submit his resignation. No one asked him to change his mind.

Winterbottom's legacy

He had done a great job in creating youth development programs all over the country but he was being paid to run the England football team and over a twelve-year time period, he had done absolutely nothing to improve any player or the performance of the team. He cannot claim to have produced one young player who has gone on to have a lengthy career with England. He was slow to realize Bobby Charlton's talent. He ignored him in the

1958 World Cup, when we failed to win one game, and in 1962, he was one of the few players he singled out for criticism, saying his ball control wasn't good enough and he was losing possession too often. This is the player who went on to play over one hundred times for England and become England's all-time record goal scorer, (until beaten by Wayne Rooney and, more recently, Harry Kane) but, most of Charlton's goals were scored after Walter had gone.

Blind faith in Walter

Yes, Hungary had taught England a lesson, but unfortunately it wasn't a good enough lesson to get rid of the manager. It seemed the Football Association had a blind faith in Walter, maybe there was a connection there that kept him on the payroll, but how he hung onto his job during that nightmare of a period for England was an absolute miracle. *Following the Hungarian debacle, from May,1953 to May, 1955 they played thirteen games and won three, drew three and lost seven.* How can any manager survive that in a team that thirty years before had commanded absolute supremacy over world football, and there were Board members of the Football Association, who were clinging to the belief that England were still the leading nation!

Moscow Dynamo completed their tour unbeaten. They had drawn 3-3 with Chelsea, beaten Arsenal 4-3, beaten Cardiff City 10-1 and were held to a draw by Rangers 2-2. For a team who arrived, not knowing what to expect of the British teams, the quality of the playing surfaces, the reaction of the thousands who watched their matches, the tour was a phenomenal success and they must have returned home heroes.

For the record:

Over a period of seven years and 68 games:
Hungary won 57, drew 8 and lost 3. Win ratio of 84%
260 goals scored with 79 against.

The greatest run of results in the history of football.

Ferenc Puskas

Honved and Barcelona: *356 games 375 goals*
Hungary: *85 games 84 goals*

Sandor Kocsis

Honved and Barcelona: *335 games 295 goals*
Hungary: *68 games 75 goals*

Brazilian Samba

"The future of football in Brazil is secure because every young kid wants to be another Pelé."- Rivellino

Here I was standing outside the ground of Santos FC at Vila Belmiro, just five minutes from the Jose Menino Beach. I had just been sent to Santos by the Bank of London and South America and this was my first branch. I decided to go in. No security, so I walked into the playing area. The players were practicing. I spotted Pelé, who was dribbling around the other players, laughing and joking. Then I spotted fellow local legends Coutinho, Lima, Mengalvio and Gilmar, the goalie, all looking fit and confident, having just beaten Benfica and AC Milan in the Intercontinental Cup, which would make them unofficially the best team in the world. They had also succeeded in winning the *campeonato brasileiro* for the fourth time in a row. The Intercontinental Cup did not pass without controversy, the Italians claiming that Santos had bribed the referee in the second leg when Santos scored four second half goals, but then, they would, wouldn't they?

An affair of the heart

It was all fun, one big samba party, without the music although, if they had the technology, I am sure there would have been. I was to visit their ground regularly and came to see their home games, and it was good to experience the extraordinary passion of the fans, something I had never witnessed before, but the Brazilians are peaceful people. It was nothing like we had witnessed in Argentina, where players and referees had been threatened. There, it was a matter of life and death. Here, in Brazil, it was more of a love affair with occasional altercations as with any affair of the heart.

Meio de campo

At the start of any friendly game, or kickabout, in Brazil, there was always a scramble for positions as everyone wants to be meio de campo, or meio-campista, the position in the centre of midfield, much like a quarterback in American football. These positions had been held for the national team, around that time by Gerson, Didi and much later, Falcao, players with a vision, together with, of course, impeccable ball control. Most plays start with the meio de campo.

Early days

The Brazilians took longer to attract visiting teams from Europe and the earlier ones all went to the River Plate countries, but Chelsea played four games in Rio and Sao Paulo, in 1929, and failed to win any of them. In the 1930 World Cup, they succeeded in winning one game against Bolivia 4-0, at the Centenario Stadium in Montevideo, a tournament in which they celebrated the first of many legends, Preguinho, who scored three goals in the tournament and one hundred and twenty goals for his club, Fluminense. There is a statue of him at Fluminense's ground in Rio de Janeiro.

Brazil on top for eighty years

In the 1934 World Cup in Italy, they lost their first game to Spain and went home early. The 1938 World Cup in France was the first one where the Brazilians made any impact, and they won the first two matches, including a 6-5 win against Poland, before losing 2-1 to the eventual winners, Italy, in the semi-final. The Brazilians were on their way, and, apart from 1966, were to play a prominent role in every World Cup, right up to 2022, so in total, they were one of the leading teams for every tournament for the next eighty years. There has been no let up. Every year, Brazil has been able to produce the most talented players in the world.

Leonidas, one of first World Cup stars

In the 1938 World Cup, Brazil had produced one of the all-time great South American players, Leonidas, who scored seven goals in the tournament and a total of twenty-one for his country in nineteen games and two hundred and thirty for Flamengo and Sao Paulo, right up to 1950. In the defeat of Poland, he scored four goals, the most for any player in a World Cup, until Just Fontaine scored four for France in 1958.

Moacyr's nightmare

In the 1950 World Cup, there was heart-ache. They were playing in front of their passionate fans and they knew it was their biggest opportunity, but somehow, the Gods were against it, as, for Brazilians, religion rules everything and for some reason it was not to be as Moacyr Barbosa, their goalkeeper, was to find out. He said later, never a day went by, for the rest of his life, when he wasn't reminded of the winning goal which slipped past him. Manga, another goalkeeper, was never allowed to forget a dismal display against Portugal in 1966. It's great playing for Brazil, but it can result in a nightmare.

Pelé's legacy

Pelé had transformed Santos into the greatest team in the world almost single-handedly. In the year he first played for Brazil, when he was seventeen, he scored sixty-two goals in forty-two matches and by the time he was twenty-one, he had scored over three hundred. There are some who downplay his fame as he was playing in an easy league. It's possible to come to that conclusion, of course, as there were no Brazilian players playing in Europe at that time, but the quality of the Brazilian national teams of the World Cups of 1958, 1962 and 1966 and of course 1970, in terms of performance and entertainment was unmistakable. Some of Pele's goals were scored against weak opposition but the same can be said of most strikers.

Garrinchas everywhere

Garrincha was another legend in Brazil, but there are Garrinchas in every corner of Brazil with the pace and trickery to get past the full back. We pay two hundred thousand pounds per week to some wingers just to see them stop, look around, slow down the movement and pass the ball back to midfield. The Brazilian wingers know it is their job to get past the fullback and reach the danger zone. Whenever a European club looks to sign a winger, the best options are always Brazilians. In 2022, Brazil had Vinicius, Antony, Raphinha and Martinelli in their World Cup squad and actually gave game-time to each of them.

The dreaded fear of losing possession

In the UK, you can see thirteen and fourteen-year-olds, all aiming to be the next George Best or Jimmy Johnstone, with the same pace and control, taking on their full back, but as soon as they get within reach of the first team, they realise that to lose possession can be fatal and it becomes an obsession, and the talent has gone. Not so the Brazilians, the message they receive is to entertain and that is foremost on their minds, every time they put their boots on to play.

Mussolini's Italy

Early years for the national team

At the Arena Civica stadium, Milan on 15th May,1910, Italy played their very first international match, defeating France 6-2. Eleven days later, the Italian team travelled to Budapest and were beaten 6-1 by the Hungarian national team. There were railway networks in the Alpine region connecting Italy, Austria, France and Hungary but it must have required a twenty-hour train journey for the Italian team to arrive in Budapest and the same again for the Hungarians when they travelled to Milan for the return match the following January. Both matches were won by the Hungarians but the willingness of both teams to undergo these long journeys reflects the passion that was emerging for football in Europe and the desire for international competition, influenced by the Olympic Games of 1904 and 1908.

Tough introduction

The Italians were receiving a tough introduction to football and between 1910 and 1913, they lost nine of their initial fourteen matches. However, they were keen enough to take a team to Stockholm for the 1912 Olympic Games, with financial support from the Government. The manager of the Italian team, Vittorio Pozzo, was soon to become a legendary figure in Italian football. He was to continue managing the Italian football team on a part-time basis, until he was appointed full-time manager from 1929 until 1948.

Hugo Meisl

The referee for their first and only match against Finland was Hugo Meisl, who would make his name as coach for Austria throughout the 1930s. Also assisting the Austrian team was Jimmy Hogan, who, after failing to find suitable coaching opportunities in his homeland, undertook a number of coaching engagements with some of the leading European teams of that era.

Mussolini's appointment

Mussolini was appointed Prime Minister of Italy in 1922 and his influence over Italian football became immeasurable. His aim was to achieve national supremacy through Italy's performance in sport, in particular the Italian football team, transforming it from the whipping boys of the early 1910s to triumph in a number of international tournaments including the World Cup in the 1930s.

Italian passion for football

He used the innate passion for football of the Italian people for his own political ends. They had been beaten by France in the earlier rounds of the 1920 Olympic Games but showed an immediate improvement in the 1924 games in France, achieving significant wins against Spain and Luxembourg to reach the quarter-finals. In 1928, in Amsterdam, they defeated France, their bête noir since their first match in 1911 and then, their most impressive result, so far, a 7-1 massacre of Spain in the quarter-finals. They were eliminated by future World Cup winners, Uruguay, in a very close game in the semi-finals and cemented a highly successful tournament by defeating Egypt 11-3 in the play-off for third place. The Italian football team had responded well to Mussolini's plan to promote fascism and the match against Uruguay had attracted fifteen thousand football enthusiasts at the Olympic Stadium in Amsterdam.

South American advances

However, Mussolini and his associates had witnessed the 1928 Olympic final between Uruguay and Argentina, which went to a re-match following an initial draw and they decided that they had no chance of winning the initial World Cup to be held in Montevideo in 1930, when it was announced by FIFA the following year, especially as it was to be hosted in South America so, along with a number of other leading countries, they declined an invitation by FIFA to participate. The Uruguay v Argentina 1928 final had alerted the footballing world to the incredible advances that were being made in South American football, in particular in the River Plate countries.

The three "oriundis" poached from Argentina

Mussolini, would have ignored the 1930 World Cup, content with Italy's progress and their third-place finish in 1928. He had probably made up his mind that there was no way Italy would beat Uruguay or Argentina, playing on their home ground. However, they had made successful bid to host the World Cup in 1934, and this was Mussolini's big opportunity. To prepare the team for this historic event, he took immediate action. He poached three of Argentina's best players, from their 1930 World Cup final team, Luis Monti, Raimundo Orsi and Enrique Guaiti, all of them "oriundi," a term used at that time to describe immigrants of native ancestry. He then appointed Vittorio Pozzo, as the team manager following a successful period as technical director with his adopted club, Torino. He had managed the 1924 and 1928 Olympic teams on a part-time basis but Mussolini realised that he needed Pozzo as a full-time coach.

Stadiums

Finally, Mussolini decided that modern football stadiums were required in each major city, to serve the dual purpose of displaying to the world the progress his fascist regime was making and also to enable football to flourish in different parts of the country. Stadiums were constructed in record time in Turin, Bologna, Florence, Livorno and Rome, and this plan to decentralise World Cup venues was adopted by every future World Cup host.

Pozzo's first success

Pozzo's first success was in 1930, in the Central European International Cup, a tournament that was held from 1927 to 1960, consisting of Italy, Austria, Hungary,

Czechoslovakia and Poland with Romania and Yugoslavia joining later. It was played over three years, later to five years and ironically, the first five countries were, along with Italy, to dominate football in the 1930s.

With the stadiums all in place, the 1934 World Cup got underway with Italy defeating the USA, third placed finalists in 1930, 7-1. One of the goals, the first of many, was scored by Giuseppe Meazza, one of Italy's greatest players who scored over two hundred goals for his club Inter Milan, and thirty-three goals for his country, which still ranks him as the second highest scorer in the history of Italian football.

Following their impressive start, Italy didn't find it too easy in the next two matches with a 1-1 draw with Spain requiring a nervous 1-0 win in the replay. This was followed by a 1-0 defeat of Austria in the semi-final with the winner being scored by "oriundi" Enrique Guaiti. Also playing in this match was the highly talented Austrian striker, Matthias Sindelar.

Refereeing scandal

Mussolini made his one mistake following Italy's win in the semi-final, a decision which was to become one of the talking points of the 1934 World Cup. The referee appointed for the semi-final, Ivan Eklind, aged 29, the youngest referee to officiate a World Cup match, was then appointed for the final also. This immediately led to accusations of corruption and despite the lack of evidence, it was suggested Eklind had been summoned to meet with Mussolini before the final. No action was taken and Eklind became one of the very few referees to officiate at three World Cups, having been selected for the tournaments in 1934, 1938 and 1950.

After eighty minutes, Czechoslovakia were leading 1-0, but Italy managed to score two goals in the final ten minutes. Italy were known for their physical fitness and in key games, they usually finished the stronger team.

Pozzo's incredible achievements

Under Vittorio Pozzo's coaching, Italy won the Central European International Cup in 1930, the World Cup in 1934, the Central European International Cup again in 1935, the Olympic Games football tournament in 1936 in Berlin and he was soon to add the World Cup of 1938, in France. No national manager in the history of football has been more successful than Pozzo. In fact, no other manager has achieved his longevity with a national team, in Pozzo's case nineteen years from 1929 to 1948, finally standing down following Italy's 4-0 defeat at the hands of England, in Turin, in May, 1948, a result which Walter Winterbottom declared was his finest achievement. Pozzo, under the direction of Mussolini, funded by the Italian government, had attained unprecedented success in the 1930s. Italian football, without question, had achieved the supremacy Mussolini had planned and were unquestionably the best team in the world.

The Battle of Highbury

Pozzo will not forget one of Italy's very few defeats in
the 1930s. A match played at Arsenal's ground in
November, 1934, shortly after their victory in the World
Cup, became known as "The Battle of Highbury," when
England defeated the World Champions 3-2. Following a
defeat to Czechoslovakia, in Prague, in May, 1935, Italy
then went on an unbeaten run of thirty matches up to
November, 1939 when they lost to Switzerland 3-1 in
Zurich.

1938 World Cup

If there had been any doubt about the supremacy Italy
had achieved, it was soon dispelled in France. They
defeated the hosts and the other rising stars in World
football, Brazil and under the captaincy of Giuseppe
Meazza, Hungary, 4-2 in the final. No scandals this time
and Italy had become the first country to win the World
Cup outside its own borders. With Brazil 1n 1958 and
1962, they are the only country to have won the World
Cup in two successive seasons.

The final curtain for Mussolini

Mussolini's end was near, however, and drawn into
WWII, he became a puppet for Hitler, and was executed,
for treason, by his own people in 1945. Pozzo continued
through the war years and he came out of retirement
following the England defeat in Turin, for his final
coaching assignment at the 1948 Olympic Games in

London where his team were defeated 5-3 by Denmark in the quarter-finals – once more at Highbury!

Tragedy hits Italian football

On 27th March, 1949, Italy defeated Spain 3-1, in Madrid, the Italian team consisting of seven Torino players. On 4th May, 1949, thirty-seven days later, a tragic event took place which was to shock the football world. An aircraft carrying the Torino team, who were returning from a match against Benfica, crashed into the Basilica of Superga. Thirty-one people perished including eighteen Torino players who were on board. Torino had won four of the last five Serie A titles and had been the leading club in Italian football for some time. Vittorio Pozzo's last job for Italian football was to identify the Torino bodies. It would be a tragic moment that would haunt him for the rest of his life.

Pelé, simply the best

"There is no way of describing the impact Pelé, had on Brazilian football. He was a God to his people and a legend to the rest of the world."

No book on the World Cup could ever be written without some reference to the player who, more than anyone else, created it. The 1930, 1934, 1938, 1950 and 1954 World Cups passed by without great excitement but in 1958, in Sweden, an exceptional player emerged who was going to grace the World Cup for the next twelve years. Suddenly the World

Cup was alive, right through the 1960s until his grand finale in 1970 in Mexico when we all witnessed, in Pelé's own words, the very best of the "beautiful game," and Pelé,', during those twelve years, never once lost that captivating smile for which he was so famous.

Although we knew he was seriously ill, the news we all heard on the evening of Thursday, December 29th, 2022, was still devastating. Ever since he emerged in that 1958 World Cup as a young wonder-kid of seventeen, he has been a player of the people. He belonged to us all.

At the 1958 World Cup he took the football world by storm scoring six goals in four matches including a hat trick against France in the semi-final and two more in the final against Sweden. What we didn't know then was that he had already scored over fifty league goals for Santos, the first at the age of fifteen. In his year of World Cup baptism, in 1958, for club and country, as a 17-year-old, he amassed 75 goals in 53 matches. By the time he was twenty-one, in 1962, he had scored over 300 goals including 34 for his country. He took his club, Santos to two Intercontinental Trophies, that's the winners of the South American Championship pitted against the European Champions. No South American club had ever done this before. Some of his goals were outrageous, running 60 yards through the whole defence time after time in the same match, the ball seemingly tied to his shoe laces.

He has been a God to the Brazilian people for over sixty years, the most revered person in Brazil's history. They will be stunned, having to face life without Pelé. Brazil's favelas will also be mourning. They know that Pelé has always been one of them. He started life with nothing, not even a pair of shoes in which to play football. Brazilian kids don't need shoes. They play bare-footed and that's how they learn to control the ball.

Pelé was born in a small village called Três Corações in Minas Gerais, in the interior of Brazil. He played with lots of kids with talent but he was lucky as someone with connections in football thought he was more exceptional than the other kids and persuaded his parents to let him take Pelé to Santos at the age of fourteen. They agreed and that's where it all started. He stayed with Santos for the whole of his career, was created a National Treasure to stop him going to a European club and was on the point of retiring when out of the blue in 1974, he received an offer to play for New York Cosmos in the newly formed NASL, and, for the next three years, from 1975 to 1977, he played in front of huge crowds, all eager to get a glimpse of the footballing legend, for a while teaming up with Carlos Alberto and Franz Beckenbauer. He also played against George Best, who he graciously labelled the best player in the world. At New York Cosmos, he played 107 matches and scored 67 goals.

As a further example of the massive impact Pelé had on football, when he retired in 1977, both New York Cosmos and the entire NASL collapsed and football in the USA went into decline and their national team didn't qualify for another World Cup until 1990.

Pelé won the 1958 and 1962 World Cups, followed by a lapse in form and injury in 1966 in England but he regained his form in 1970 and was part of that amazing team of Jairsinho, Carlos Alberto, Rivellino, Clodoaldo and Tostão who won the 1970 World Cup in Mexico. He remains the only player to have won three World Cups, a unique record which surely will never be equalled.

He was not an educated man but his celebrity status and personality earned him positions in both local and federal governments. He was not at ease in politics, however, and limited his public activities to TV appearances and football-related events.

He has not been well for the last year and has been in and out of hospital for some time with colon and prostate issues. In the end old age caught up with him and he died peacefully at a hospital in São Paulo with family and friends at his side.

When I lived in Brazil, I watched him play for Santos on several occasions and I discovered that he was also an amazing person who never stopped smiling and who always had time for other people. He was a God to his colleagues and also his opponents, who often had too much respect to tackle him and lived in fear of injuring him.

No one in football deserves the name "King" more than Pelé. He was simply the best. The number 10 shirt will be his forever. R.I.P Football legend, Edson Arantes do Nascimento aka "Pelé"

Paul Hawkins

Acknowledgements

The motivation to write a book usually comes from the author's own drive and energy. In my case I could not have finished this project without the encouragement of friends and family so I would like to thank:

My family, Liz, Suzi, Stevie, little Georgie for their patience and understanding and allowing me the time and space to complete the project.

Patrick and Clare for their motivational feedback at all times.

My brilliant graphic designer Mushafiq Ashai for her innovative and creative design work

Ed Smith and Simon Martin, Course Directors for the History of Sport Degree Course at Buckingham University which provided the motivation to take up writing again.

The brilliant people at the British Society for Sports History (BSSH) whose conferences were so motivational.

The fine people at the North American Sports Society History (NASSH) in Chicago, whose conference at Boise, Idaho, was an unforgettable experience.

Dr Gary James whose International Football Conference at Manchester City Football Academy provided inspiration and encouragement.

Printed in Great Britain
by Amazon

25404721R00109